Lost Writings

of

Howard Weeden

as

"Flake White"

Compiled and Edited by

Sarah Huff Fisk

and

Linda Wright Riley

Big Spring Press, Inc.
Huntsville, Alabama

ISBN: 0-9765836-0-7
Library of Congress Control Number: 2005920921

First Edition

Cover design by Evelyn Wright and Chuck Rogers
Text format by Angi Christo

Published by: Big Spring Press, Inc.
                 P.O. Box 292
                 Huntsville, AL 35804-0292

Production by Colonial Graphics Group

Printed in the United States of America

Table of Contents

Christmas   157

Fables   195

Acknowledgements

We only know into what waters we drop the stone. We never know to what far and lovely shore the ripples may reach.

—Howard Weeden [Flake White]
"Household Decoration" 1882

Howard Weeden as "Flake White" reaches the shore of the 21st century through the efforts of many people who love history and are happy to share it. We thank Margaret Belle Crow and Perky Taylor of the Huntsville Pilgrimage Association who invited us a few years ago to become "players" in our city's history at Maple Hill's Cemetery Stroll. As Howard Weeden's impersonator, Linda quickly sought Sarah Fisk's remembrance of several 1956 interviews that she and other members of Huntsville's Culture Club had conducted with Weeden's close friend, Miss Elizabeth Price. In them, Price recalled that Weeden's early writings as "Flake White" appeared in the Presbyterian *Christian Observer*…! Suddenly, our "parts to play" in the story of Howard Weeden became a four-year quest that depended on many other players.

We are most grateful to Dr. Edwin P. Elliott, editor of the present-day *Christian Observer,* who encouraged our desire to preserve from the *Observer's* heritage such a remarkable voice as Howard Weeden's. We are indebted to Rick Jones and Angela G. Morris of the E. M. White Library, Louisville Presbyterian Theological Seminary, who welcomed us into their "vault" of priceless bound volumes of this old newspaper. Eileen Sklar, Margery N. Sly and William B. Bynum of the Presbyterian Historical Society's libraries in Philadelphia and Montreat also opened their special collections to us.

Acknowledgments

Closer to home, we had first learned how to locate the *Observer* through the helpfulness of Raneé Pruitt and others in the Heritage Room of the Huntsville-Madison County Public Library. This led us to Nashville where, assisted by Rachel Adams of the Vanderbilt Interlibary Loan Office, we identified the few libraries housing the *Observer.* Emily Saile accompanied us to the Louisville Presbyterian Theological Seminary where, over a period of days, we made most of our discoveries. We then cross-referenced Weeden's publications in the *Observer* with contemporaneous Huntsville papers that are archived in the Madison County Records Center, enabled by Rhonda Larkin and Donna Dunham.

Barbara Lauster, Director of the Weeden House Museum, shared some early Weeden paintings that reflect the artist's "Flake White" period. We were encouraged by the reception of our manuscript by Dr. William G. Cockrill and Paula Brown of the First Presbyterian Church. Also, we appreciated the enthusiasm for our book expressed by Randy Roper of the Twickenham Historic Preservation District Association. In addition, we thank Jack Burwell, Pat Robertson and Stephanie Timberlake of Burritt Museum for their help in reproducing other early Weeden paintings in this collection.

For their helpfulness, we thank Dr. John Rison Jones, John Shaver, and Nancy Rohr of the Huntsville-Madison County Historical Society. Special thanks go to Emily Burwell for her diligent proofing of our manuscript. Others giving assistance were Tina Grant, Ann Hammond, Emily Saile, Anne Swain and Cherry Trimble.

Finally, and most especially, we thank our families, Emily Saile and Kerry Pinkerton, Ken and Elizabeth Riley, and Evelyn and the late Whit Wright for their tremendous support of us and our project.

Sarah Huff Fisk and Linda Wright Riley

Introduction

Finding "Flake White"

Long before writing her first book *Shadows on the Wall* in 1898, Maria Howard Weeden published numerous other writings using the pseudonym "Flake White." For thirty years, she wrote under a different name and with an identity practically unknown to her present-day admirers. From 1866 to 1896, the deeply Christian and highly sophisticated voice of Miss Howard Weeden travelled across many states and into thousands of homes to speak to families subscribing to such weekly newspapers as the *Christian Observer*, the Huntsville *Democrat*, the Huntsville *Independent*, and the Huntsville *Argus*. She was known to her readers as simply "Flake White" of Huntsville, Alabama.

Prior to now, the writings of "Flake White" have never been collected or published beyond their author's lifetime, probably because Weeden herself did not seek to republish them. Rather, she devoted the last decade of her life to a new and all-consuming interest, that of creating four volumes of portraits and verse dedicated to a vanishing generation of people whose history was important in the American South. The publication of these volumes[1] was met with great success, such that before her death in 1905, Weeden had achieved international recognition as the artist responsible for hundreds of exquisite portraits of African Americans living in and near Huntsville, Alabama during the post-Civil War Reconstruction period.[2] Howard Weeden signed her real name to these works, and it is with them that she is most readily associated. Thus overshadowed by an accomplishment so significant, the writings of "Flake White" have lain dormant for over 100 years.

Finding these treasures would present no easy task, even for those who have long known of their existence. Only a few of the original clippings attributed to "Flake White" are archived in the Howard Weeden collection;[3] and no comprehensive bibliography of Weeden's pseudonymous writings has been preserved. Knowing only that Howard Weeden had written for the Presbyterian newspaper, the *Christian Observer*, using a pen name during the late 1860's, our quest became to find and examine any surviving originals of this publication–in search of "Flake White."

Our pursuit led us to three repositories for this historic religious periodical. They are the E. M. White Library of

---

[1] *Shadows on the Wall* (1898); *Bandanna Ballads* (1899); *Songs of the Old South* (1901); and *Old Voices* (1904).

[2] Sarah Huff Fisk and Frances C. Roberts, *Shadows on the Wall: The Life and Works of Howard Weeden* (Huntsville: Burritt Museum, 1962) 22-23.

[3] Howard Weeden Collection (Huntsville-Madison County Public Library).

the Louisville Presbyterian Theological Seminary, and the libraries of the Presbyterian Historical Society located in Philadelphia, Pennsylvania and Montreat, North Carolina, each holding partial collections of the *Christian Observer*. At these libraries, we spent many hours perusing the crumbling pages of hundreds of weekly issues of a periodical that was a household word to Presbyterian families during the nineteenth century. Originally founded in 1813 as the *Religious Remembrancer* in Philadelphia, the mission of the *Christian Observer* was to provide moral and spiritual edification for the whole family. Its pages offered a variety of religious articles including theological essays, biblical exegeses, biographical sketches, discourses on godly living, and church news, as well as stories, letters and poems.[4]

Subscription records indicate that the Weeden family had subscribed to the *Christian Observer* for 80 years, beginning in 1833.[5] Owned and edited by the Amasa Converse family for over three generations, the newspaper's offices relocated from Philadelphia to Richmond, Virginia in 1861, and from there moved to Louisville, Kentucky in 1869.[6] During Howard Weeden's

---

[4] Jean Hoornstra and Trudy Heath, eds., *American Periodicals 1741-1900: An Index to the Microfilm Collections* (Ann Arbor: UMI Co.) Title Index 57-58.

[5] "Roll of Long Time Subscribers to the *Christian Observer*," *Christian Observer Centennial Edition*, 3 September 1913:19. Converse Family Papers, box 4, Presbyterian Historical Society, Montreat, N.C.

[6] "A Century and a Quarter of Publication of the *Christian Observer* by the Converse Family," *Christian Observer*, 20 February 1952:2.

association with the paper, the *Christian Observer* was generally recognized as the medium for communication for the United Synod of Southern Presbyteries.[7] While the paper enjoyed a circulation of 3,000 in 1876,[8] its readership had tripled by 1886 to 10,777.[9] Surviving financial records for the self-supporting paper show no payments being made to its writing contributors[10] who included some of the most erudite and well-respected preachers in the presbyteries. Many articles, especially prior to the 1880's, were signed with pseudonyms or with mere localities, and often with no names at all.

The *Christian Observer* would have been a natural choice for young Howard Weeden to send her manuscripts for publication. She grew up in a home where weekly issues of the newspaper were treasured as a source of "good news" and presented to others by her mother, Jane Weeden.[11] Also, officers of Howard's own home church (the Presbyterian Church of Huntsville, now known as the

---

[7]   "Dr. Amasa Converse," *Christian Observer,* 3 September 1913:8.

[8]   See footnote 5.

[9]   "Circulation of the *Christian Observer,* July 1, 1886," Converse Family Papers, box 1, "Circulation" folder, Presbyterian Historical Society, Montreat, N.C.

[10] "Statement of the Finances of the *Christian Observer* : July 1, 1877 to June 30, 1878," Converse Family Papers, box 1, "Finances" folder, Presbyterian Historical Society, Montreat, N.C.

[11] Howard Weeden [Flake White], "A Saturday Mission," *Christian Observer*, 8 July 1885:1.

First Presbyterian Church) subscribed to and even wrote for the paper.[12]

When Howard Weeden was nineteen years old, she made her first known appearance as "Flake White" in the *Christian Observer* on February 8, 1866 with a short story entitled "Patience." The following week, February 16, the same "Flake White" contributed a strikingly different essay on "Modern Fashions" to her hometown paper, the Huntsville Daily *Independent*. Together, the story and essay foreshadow the remarkably mature and versatile voice of Maria Howard Weeden who will speak throughout this collection. In "Patience" she tells a simple, moralistic story to edify young Christian readers. In "Modern Fashions" she amuses and illuminates her more temporal readers by describing what is "ancient" about "modern" fashions. Soon after the publication of these pieces, eight more short stories by "Flake White" appear in the *Christian Observer*—all before the end of the year 1866.[13]

That was no ordinary year in the life of Howard Weeden, who, with her mother and sister Kate had only recently returned from Tuskegee where they lived as

[12] Samuel Coltart, an elder in the church from 1851-1873, is listed as a subscriber in 1858 ("Accounts Sent Out by the *Observer*," Converse Family Papers, box 1, Presbyterian Historical Society, Montreat, N.C.). As well, Dr. Fred A. Ross, the preacher from 1855-1875, co-edited the *Calvinistic Magazine* (later called the *Presbyterian Witness*) that united with the *Christian Observer* in 1858 ("The Oldest Religious Newspaper in the World," *Christian Observer*, 6 September 1893).

[13] Their dates: February 22, April 5, April 19, May 3, June 4, August 30, September 6, and October 25.

refugees during the Civil War and Huntsville's occupation by Federal troops. The difficulties that they faced in reclaiming their home and in trying to resume their previous lifestyle are surprisingly absent from Weeden's choice of topics. This would suggest that these early stories may have been written and unpublished prior to the family's return to Huntsville, during her days as a student at Tuskegee Female College where essay writing and earnest study of the English classics were routine.[14]

Having entered the school in September of 1862 and graduated in May of 1865, Weeden would have certainly reaped the influence of two extraordinary scholars of English literature. They were the first two presidents of the college: Dr. Andrew A. Lipscomb (1856-1859), and his good friend Dr. George W. F. Price (1859-1863, 1865-1872). Both were beloved Methodist ministers of highly cultivated intellect, known for their exceptional writing, speaking and teaching abilities. Although Dr. Lipscomb left the college in 1860 to become the president of the University of Georgia, his personality and pedagogy left an indelible imprint on Tuskegee Female College during the tenure of Dr. George Price, his successor.[15]

Dr. Lipscomb, who had imparted to his students a great love of Shakespeare, Milton, Addison, Johnson and others, was himself a prolific contributing writer to many religious and literary magazines, including the prestigious *Harper's New Monthly Magazine*. In his over fifty-one articles written for this periodical, Dr. Lipscomb reveals his

---

[14] Rhoda C. Ellison, *History of Huntingdon College: 1854-1954* (Montgomery: Huntingdon College, 2004) 10-32.

[15] Ibid., 10-14; 38-40; 79.

passionate advocacy for the education of young women, and his Christian idealism as it pertains to one's relationship with the world. Weeden very likely read Lipscomb's writings, as the magazine was assigned reading material in Dr. Price's literature classes.[16] Although we find no direct reference to Lipscomb in our collection of Weeden's writings, certain qualities of her own personality are mirrored in the character traits that he extols in his articles. For example, in his essay on "The Cultivation of the Ideal," Lipscomb describes Nature from the perspective of the artist or idealist:

> A man of true sympathy can not lay his hand on a weed and not feel a divine pulse throbbing in it. Nature will be idealized. She is not Nature unless idealized. And whether by poetry or devotion, whether by the art peculiar to genius or by those means which are in the hands of all, she is idealized whenever her real offices are apprehended. Every man who finds companionship and joy in natural objects is an idealist. He becomes an idealist by the act that raises nature above the barren idea of machinery, and conforms it to a spiritual purpose….Let us not suppose, then, that artists and poets are the only persons interested in the cultivation of the ideal. It is the want of our common nature….All of us must have a better world than the actual world around us, and hence the kindness of nature provides the far-reaching avenue of thought and fancy, through

[16]   Ibid., 13-30.

which the spirit makes its escape and luxuriates in the boundlessness of its power....Ideality, then, is....nothing less than the immortal mind adjusting itself to those objects which lie above the vicissitudes of circumstance.[17]

As an artist of wildflowers, local scenery, and ultimately of people, Howard Weeden did indeed spiritualize her acquaintance with all of Nature. With her brush, she elevated the lowliest flower, and reflected the dignity of the humblest servant. Similarly, with her pen, "Flake White" rose above the vicissitudes of real life that Weeden surely must have experienced during and after the Civil War. She chose subjects having amazingly nothing to do with slavery, the war, or its aftermath. Most of her stories are set in imaginary settings, with little to identify them with her hometown. Her stories and themes reside in a different place.

Instead of dwelling on her own circumstances, Weeden employed her tender sensibilities to "lift up" the faithful. Written in the religiously overt, Victorian style of her day, "Flake White's" simple stories and fables reassure her readers of the heavenly reward awaiting those who, in repentance, embrace the cross of Christ to find a refuge in times of trial. She venerates the humble and disciplined lives of her characters who find their greatest joy in serving and sacrificing for others. She sympathizes with the orphaned, the lame, the poor, the persecuted, and champions the blessed ones who express love, charity and service to the weak.

---

[17] A. A. Lipscomb, "The Cultivation of the Ideal," *Harper's New Monthly Magazine,* October 1859:700-702.

It is little wonder that, in her youth, Howard Weeden would choose "Flake White" as her pseudonym for writings meant to inspire others to higher ground. Studying oil painting first under William Frye[18] in Huntsville, then Julia Spear[19] in Tuskegee, she learned great respect for flake white, an old-fashioned white pigment known for centuries to have the unsurpassed qualities of durability and opacity.[20] The old masters such as Titian, Rubens and Vermeer all used flake white to cast the warm, glowing highlights in their paintings.

So, too, does the heart of Howard Weeden as "Flake White" glow from the pages of her essays. In them, she writes gently yet boldly about "things eternal," even as she describes such topics as her mother's weekly "mission"; the wonder of optimism; the fall of Eve; the vanity of fashion; the imagination of children; the transcendence of hymns; the passion of revivalists and foreign workers; and the artistry of others.

Never have Howard Weeden's personal convictions and imaginings resounded more clearly or with such authority and wit, subtlety and grace than now—as we turn, for the first time, through the pages of "Flake White's" essays. And as we do, we discover how writing under a pseudonym afforded Weeden more than just a running celestial theme. It gave her the anonymity needed to honestly speak as her faith and heart led her. Imagine a Southern, genteel lady of the nineteenth century openly challenging a man in print,

[18] Fisk and Roberts, *Shadows on the Wall*, 8.
[19] Ellison, *History of Huntingdon College 1854-1954*, 50.
[20] Ralph Mayer, *The Artist's Handbook of Materials and Techniques*, 4th ed. (New York: Viking Press, 1981) 93-94.

and a learned theologian at that. Howard Weeden would not be so bold; but "Flake White" could be, in her "Letter to a D. D."[21] What sport we find in this writer's persona!

Moreover, what breadth we see in Weeden's education, as she frequently draws from her "palette" full of literary, biblical and historical allusions. (The writer's pseudonym naturally permits her to do this, all the while retaining her personal modesty, a highly important feminine virtue in her day.) With prose that is often nothing short of dazzling, this artist of the mid-nineteenth century entreats us to hear the minds and voices that enlightened her: voices such as Moses, William Shakespeare, John Milton, Isaac Watts, William Hazlitt, Samuel Coleridge, Charlotte Elliott, Andrew Young, Victor Hugo, Ralph Waldo Emerson, Hans Christian Andersen, Elizabeth Barrett Browning, Alfred Lord Tennyson, John Ruskin, George Eliot, Horatio Alger and many others.

Occasionally, Howard Weeden invited her own Huntsville community to read what "Flake White" wrote for the *Christian Observer*.[22] On July 1, 1875 when the Huntsville Weekly *Democrat* reprinted her literary critique on Elizabeth Barrett Browning's "A Drama of Exile," the Huntsville editor wrote of the article:

---

[21] Howard Weeden [Flake White], "Rev. Sam Jones at Huntsville: Letter to a D. D.," *Christian Observer,* 18 February 1885:5.

[22] "Mrs. Browning's Eve," Huntsville Weekly *Democrat*, 1 July 1875; "Rev. Sam Jones at Huntsville: Letter to a D. D.," Huntsville Weekly *Independent*, 26 February 1886; "Moody and Sankey at Selma, Ala.," Huntsville Weekly *Independent*, 1 April 1886.

MRS. BROWNING'S 'EVE' —The critique with the above title, on our first page, was contributed to the *Christian Observer* by our gifted and accomplished townswoman, MISS HOWARD WEEDEN. A devotee of Art and Literature, with native aesthetic capacity and tastes, carefully cultivated by study and practice, she has a keen perception of the beauties of Nature, Art and Science, and a ready and skillful pen to describe them, and pencil to paint them, as well as the bright and beautiful creations of her own fruitful fancy.[23]

Early in her life, Howard Weeden was enamored for her writing as well as for her art. As a young painter living in a century when few women writers revealed their identities, she chose from among the "colors" of her palette the name "Flake White" to bear her "bright and beautiful creations" to readers young and old. Though she wrote in an old-fashioned way, her voice speaks to every generation of the timeless virtues of faith, hope, and love.

---

[23] "Mrs. Browning's 'Eve'," Huntsville Weekly *Democrat*, 1 July 1875.

Editorial Note

This collection consists of over 40 newspaper writings by Maria Howard Weeden (1846-1905), most of which were published under her pseudonym "Flake White." They are reproduced here with the bylines just as they appeared in the original newspapers. By the mid-1890's, Weeden began publishing under her own name as did many women writers of this time.

All titles except four were addressed to and published by the *Christian Observer*. The four exceptions were published by various Huntsville newspapers and are so identified on their title pages.

For clarity, we have corrected typographical errors and have normalized spelling, punctuation and occasional sentence structures. Where helpful, we have provided editorial notes to some of the essays, as well as footnotes for literary and historical references.

Although none of these writings were originally illustrated, several of Weeden's paintings are reproduced in this collection alongside writings that seem to correspond. These include her watercolor illumination of a quotation from Horatio Alger (page 6), and two oil paintings, the "Head of a Steer" (page 142) and the "Courier of the Desert" (page 196). Unless otherwise designated, all other illustrations are from newspapers and magazines of the period.

Essays

Christian Observer Centennial Edition, 3 September 1913.

Described as the "oldest religious newspaper in the world," the *Christian Observer* originated in 1813 as the *Religious Remembrancer* and remains in publication to the present day.

A Saturday Mission

By Flake White

I do not think in all her life that my mother ever destroyed a religious paper. She thought that unlike short-lived secular papers, they did not lose value when their dates lost freshness, but became tracts when they ceased to be "news" papers, knowing the best news[1] in them to be already 1800 years old.

For this reason, the most iconoclastic member of the household respected the fresh *Christian Observers*[2] and *Southwesterns*[3] that lay in her workbasket, and spared with equal reverence the

---

[1] "I bring you good tidings of great joy, which shall be to all people. For unto you is born this day in the city of David a Saviour, which is Christ the Lord" (Luke 2:10-11, King James Version).

[2] A leading Presbyterian weekly newspaper published originally from Philadelphia in 1813, but later moved to Richmond then Louisville, where it was owned and edited by the Amasa Converse family.

[3] A Presbyterian weekly published from New Orleans (1868-1908).

past week's numbers that gathered on the table ready for her Saturday mission. Saturday was market day in our country town; the day when "Birnam came to Dunsinane,"[4] when men and boys from the caves and mountains brought their wild, sweet products in; the day when trade was not across counters, but in homes, when these rustic vendors and the lady of the house made their kindly bargains with a mingling of large and pleasant humanness. I remember the tall, rough mountaineer coming in with his full-freighted panniers,[5] measuring out their contents as my mother dictated, and carefully depositing the coins she gave him into his little leather purse.

Then (if one of her accustomed vendors) he would pause a perceptible instant before turning away—an instant in which she would hand him one of those religious papers, and which he would take with such an air of its being part of the performance, that I thought it was! This was my sole childish experience in "trade," and it gave me an abiding belief that in all traffic this preliminary exchange of goods for money was followed by some such benediction, and though I learned differently in time, the world's barter has been sweeter for such a memory.

---

[4]   When the forest of Birnam Wood actually "comes," as men carrying branches, to the castle of Dunsinane in Shakespeare's play, *Macbeth* (Act 5, Scene 5).

[5]   A pair of baskets hung across a mule for carrying produce.

Hers was not an exercise of charity; these mountaineers were naturally grave and reserved of speech. And I doubt if their kind benefactress had many thanks, or was ever gladdened by hearing the results of her work.

Nevertheless, a charity so persistently done for half a century[6] could not have been overlooked by Him who blesses when man forgets. These papers went into lonely caves and remote mountain places, where Sabbath bells did not ring, where books were almost unknown and wholly unwelcome. But newspapers had a charm for these people, as they have for all men, and divine truths may be made to reach such souls through papers, when they would not be accepted through tracts or books—as a missionary gets a Japanese to read the Decalogue,[7] if printed on his fan.

I heard the other day of the death of one of these old pensioners—gone from his lonely mountain home to a better one, the way to which was lighted, we know not how brightly, by my mother's papers.

[8 July 1885]

---

[6]   In 1885, when this article was published, the Weedens had subscribed to the *Christian Observer* for 52 years; thus, for half a century ("Roll of Long Time Subscribers to the *Christian Observer*," *Christian Observer*, 3 September 1913:19).

[7]   The Ten Commandments (Exodus 20:2-17).

Courtesy of The Weeden House Museum

"God hands gifts to some, whispers them to others."
–Horatio Alger
by
Howard Weeden

WHISPERED GIFTS

A happy little conceit has taken form from art lately, in a statuette called the "Fairy's Whisper." It represents a child, sitting with wrapt, visionary face, listening to a fairy whispering in its ear.

The conceit charms us, because in a certain way we all acknowledge its truth, since it repeats the creed taught us in our fairy-tale days. There exist certain mortals favored with visits from fairy-folk, who, instead of leaving them gifts of gold and gems, choose to drop into their ears magic words from the other world. Once heard, these words are never forgotten, for they have power henceforth to change the listener's prosaic world into something like the magic one from whence they came.

It is a child's creed, but, thank God, raised heavenward, it is ours, also. Alger[1] has written in golden brevity when speaking of the mystery of

---

[1]   Horatio Alger, Jr. (1832-1899). An American writer of books whose heroes are rewarded for virtue.

benefits: "God hands gifts to some, and whispers them to others."

Did you ever think, when murmuring over the seeming merciless inequality of God's gifts, that there is really no inequality; for it is only our dull vision that enables us to see the palpable gifts, but does not permit us to recognize the impalpable? To this dull vision, for instance, there appears a cruel difference between the gifts handed the rich man, and those whispered to the content man. Thus Hamlet's was a worldly scoff when he taunted Horatio for having "no revenue but good spirits to feed and clothe him!"[2] In truth the melancholy prince, and many of his ilk, have mourned 'neath loads of gold to wear in their bosoms the herb called hearts-ease.[3]

One who knew the inability of gold to buy happiness has said that it is better "for a man to be born with a fixed disposition always to look on the bright side of things than to be born to ten thousand a year."[4] And to this may be added a twin gift—the capacity to look on the *beautiful* side of things—the wondrous power that can make the sight of a daisy lift a ploughman into a poet. The same gift teaches us to approach all nature from its "golden side," till the curse seems

---

[2] *Hamlet, Prince of Denmark,* Act 3, Scene 2 (c. 1601) by William Shakespeare (1564-1616).

[3] Hearts-ease: peace of mind, or tranquility.

[4] David Hume (1711-1776). A Scottish philosopher and historian.

lifted from earth, and the "Gate Beautiful"[5] opens wide as the poles.

Most of us, perhaps, have felt a sense of baffled wonder at the dull people to whom the gift of travel in search of the beautiful is often given, above the appreciative ones left at home—but the law of compensation rules here, too. As Curtis[6] says, "One man goes four thousand miles to see Italy, and does not see it—he is so shortsighted; another is so farsighted he stays in his room and sees more than Italy."

Let us not then fight with "iron laws in the end found golden,"[7] but trust Him, "whose meanest gifts put man's best dreams to shame."[8]

[29 July 1874]   FLAKE WHITE

---

5   To the heavenly "New Jerusalem" (Rev. 21:10, 25; 22:3, 14).

6   George W. Curtis (1824-1892). An American writer who held that wealth is not necessary for happiness (*Prue & I*, 1856).

7   From *The Princess*, IV (1847) by Alfred Lord Tennyson (1809-1892).

8   From *Sonnets from the Portuguese*, XXVI (1850) by Elizabeth Barrett Browning (1806-1861).

Editorial Note

On July 1, 1875, the Huntsville Weekly *Democrat* identified Miss Howard Weeden as the writer of "Miss Browning's 'Eve'," an article originally published under the name "Flake White" in the *Christian Observer* on June 16, 1875. The *Democrat* wrote:

MRS. BROWNING'S "EVE" —The critique with the above title, on our first page, was contributed to the *Christian Observer* by our gifted and accomplished townswoman, MISS HOWARD WEEDEN. A devotee to Art and Literature, with native aesthetic capacity and tastes, carefully cultivated by study and practice, she has a keen perception of the beauties of Nature, Art and Science, and a ready and skillful pen to describe them, and pencil to paint them, as well as the bright and beautiful creations of her own fruitful fancy. In her criticism of Mrs. Browning's "Eve," she exhibits a rare justness of discrimination and accuracy of judgement; a masculine grasp of the subject, combined with a feminine grace, delicacy and softness of touch in handling it....Thus appreciating Miss Weeden's critique on a chef d'oeuvres of one of the most gifted of English poets, we have transferred it to our columns with pride and pleasure. Mrs. Browning might well afford to have her beauties reflected by so bright and faithful a mental mirror, and pen-pictured by so appreciative and skillful an artist.

Elizabeth Barrett Browning (1806-1861)

MRS. BROWNING'S "EVE"

Milton's "Paradise Lost"[1] has long since put on its immortality and been translated by its own merit to a place beyond the power to censure or applause to elevate. It will stand in austere calf and grave morocco on the shelves of simple men and scholars till books are no more, and simple men and scholars will forever have their words of praise for the glimpses of bright and solemn splendors its pages reveal. Meanwhile, there is small disloyalty in choosing to turn sometimes from its secure fame to another story of the fall,

---

[1]   *Paradise Lost* (1677) by John Milton (1608-1674). Considered one of the greatest epic poems ever written, it is about the fall of Adam and Eve from the garden of Eden.

as left us in Mrs. Browning's "A Drama of Exile,"[2] in which, if there are many things that Milton would not have written, there is one thing—the beautiful character of its "Eve"—that he *could not* have written.

Milton's "Eve" is a goddess!—sufficient reason why he must needs drop the curtain upon her when she fell. An epic heroine, whose person is moulded in grand proportion, who speaks in sonorous rhetoric, of whom some womanly things are said and manly things proved, can be interesting only as the heroine of Paradise, and would make but a sorry show as a fallen goddess.

Mrs. Browning's "Eve" is a woman—a woman whom "sorrow has made more beautiful than beauty's self," presented to us in the attitude most touching to humanity, her character for suffering.

Her story does not open till after the fall, when we meet her standing outside the gate of Eden, an exile—and behold how close she stands to Adam!—closer because of his wretchedness, therein illustrating that heavenliest quality left in woman, her touching sympathy with grief and instinctive allegiance to sorrow. Adam is uncrowned, but he is "her king, if not the world's."

"Adam loves Eve—Jehovah pardons both." Thus has love simplified the plan of her life, and henceforth it is her woman's right to stand

---

2   *A Drama of Exile* (1844), by Elizabeth Barrett Browning (1806-1861), tells the story of the fall from the perspective of Eve.

nearest him—nearest in weal, perhaps, in woe of a surety!

Manlike, Adam stands for a little space more shaken by his banishment than Eve, and it is she who first makes bold to step across the sword-glare into the dangers of their future, with the unhesitating sort of courage that has made Lamartine[3] say of women, they are more heroic than heroes. Mrs. Browning's delicate perception of that "most illogical, irrational nature of womanhood," saves her from the fault of remaining heroic. For this Eve, not being epic, presently loses courage, when night, awful night out of Eden approaches, and fear falling upon her like a curse, she cries—

> I am afraid—afraid;
> I think it is God's will to make me afraid!

This is a stroke of womanly character, true as nature and sorrowful as life.

So stands this Eve, "fresh with nature's daybreak on her face,"[4] yet, familiar as your wife, sir!—true type of her daughters. Very fair to look upon, easily moved to sin, quickly and deeply forced to repent, weak in prosperity, strong in adversity, a siren in pleasure, an evangel in grief, willful in joy, obedient in sorrow, timid in small doubts, strong in desperate moments—she is the

---

[3]   Alphonse Marie Louis de Lamartine (1790-1869). A French romantic poet and writer.

[4]   From *Aurora Leigh*, Second Book (1864) by E. B. Browning.

paradox of nature, the mystery of creation, over whose rights and wrongs, equality, education and avocations, men have puzzled themselves since time began, and which Adam clears at a bound in this beautiful apostrophe to Eve:

Rise, woman, rise
To thy peculiar and best altitudes,
Of doing good and enduring ill,
Of comforting for ill, and teaching good,
And reconciling all that ill and good
Unto the patience of a constant hope—
Rise with thy daughters! If sin came by
thee,
And by sin, death; the ransom-righteousness,
The heavenly life and compensative rest
Shall come by means of thee.
Be satisfied;
Something thou hast to bear through
womanhood—
Peculiar suffering answering to the sin—
Some pang paid down for each new
human life,
Some weariness in guarding such a life,
Some coldness from the guarded,
some mistrust
From those thou hast too well served;
from those beloved
Too loyally, some treason; feebleness
Within thy heart, and cruelty without,
And pressures of an alien tyranny
With its dynastic reasons of larger bones
And stronger sinews. But go to! thy love
Shall chant itself its own beatitudes

After its own life-working. A child's kiss,
Set on thy sighing lips, shall make thee glad;
A poor man, served by thee, shall make thee
          rich;
A sick man, helped by thee, shall make thee
          strong.
Thou shalt be served thyself by every sense
Of service which thou renderest. Such a
          crown
I set upon thy head.

To which Eve answers:
                    I accept
For me and for my daughter this high part
Which lowly shall be counted. Noble work
Shall hold me in the place of garden-rest,
And in the place of Eden's lost delight,
Worthy endurance of permitted pain;
While on my longest patience there shall wait,
Death's speechless angel, smiling in the east,
Whence cometh the cold wind. I bow myself
Humbly henceforth on the ill I did,
That humbleness may keep it in the shade.
Shall it be so? Shall I smile, saying so?
O, Seed! O, King! O, God, who *shalt* be seed—
What shall I say? As Eden's fountains swelled
Brightly betwixt their banks, so swells my soul
Betwixt thy love and power!

[16 June 1875]   FLAKE WHITE

For the Huntsville Daily *Independent*

MODERN FASHIONS

The mercers of fashion, as they hand out their tempting goods before the eyes of fashion worshippers, have one phrase of allurement that seldom fails to attract, the cry of "Something New!"—a fallacy constantly heard, and constantly believed, except by a thoughtful few to whom fashion is a very peddler, crying his monotonous song, "Old Clothes, Old Clothes!" Johnson says invention now is but discovery: a saying emphatically true of fashion.

The nineteenth century stands astonished before old Pompeii whose houses contain nearly all those ingenious comforts that we had before believed ours by right of advanced civilization and an age of steam. So, could we bring back from dust the sleepers in Pyramids, Sepulchers and Mausoleums, how we would start to see that we are but as shadows thrown by the ancient sun from those living long ago in the world's early morning. Our women have but to look from their present fashion-plates to the statues of antiquity to see the simplicity of styles in hair dressing: the bunch of curls at the back of the head, the short ones falling over the brow, or the bandeaux crossing the head. The belles of our age with ruffled skirts are but Chinese belles of several centuries old. And the "new style of net" is but a type of what Greek girls put their tresses in when they smiled at their beauty in mirrors of polished metal.

Hearts are gathered now in crimson cloaks and hoods, just as in that far off "once upon a time" when wild heart's-ease were gathered by Red Riding Hood. And city pavements are glided over in looped-up dresses now, as cow-slipped meadows once were by peasant girls, and for the striped skirts worn under them, we have only to turn to the year 1777 when the Union came out in her bunting balmoral of red and white. Our lofty headdresses are but repetitions of those worn by Maria Antoinette[1] and the women of her day. And for our waterfalls! Atlas,[2] with the world upon his shoulders, stands as a great first cause of the style that now loads dainty shoulders with a world of hair!

A striking peculiarity of modern fashion is its sphinx-like character. Every fashionably dressed woman is a very riddle. "Is this," she asks, "a hat

---

[1]   Maria Antoinette (1755-1793). Queen of France, wife of Louis XVI.

[2]   A god in Greek mythology.

or a bonnet?" We waver, change ideas like a politician, and leave it undecided. "Or is it a Scotch bonnet or a Turkish turban, or a bouquet-holder, or a bird's nest?" Then the bird-mummy perched on the edge of a very nest-like affair brings us triumphantly to the latter opinion. "Is this my cloak or my husband's coat?" We cannot hazard a reply. "Are these his boots or mine?" The absence of a spur inclines us to the last opinion, while the presence at the top of the boot of red tassels tells us that jesters in motley apparel are now wearing fools caps on their feet, instead of their heads.

[16 February 1866]   Flake White

Image from the Huntsville Weekly *Mercury,* 1 February 1893

A Plea For Pinafores

The growing taste of the present day for a revival of fashions belonging to former ages is looked upon by many practical progressionists as a sort of Lot's wife[1] habit, the past being to them Sodom, and the present with its steam and electricity—in very truth—the age of progress which may grasp something from the future, perhaps, but which can borrow nothing from the past.

To them the cry for old china, Gothic furniture, medieval pictures and antique statues is unpardonable and incomprehensible paganism, but to even the most progressive of minds, there is one sunny old fashion whose claim is always acknowledged—and that is for old-fashioned children.

Who would not deem it a privilege to see once more a generation of children with "Nature's daybreak in their faces" who are less old, learned, priggish and blasé than these about us, who escaping the general spirit of forced maturity, pass slowly through a genuine chubby childhood and a simple unhastened youth?

---

[1] Upon fleeing the destruction of Sodom, Lot's wife looked back. As a result, she was turned into a pillar of salt (Genesis 19:26).

The longest childhood permitted is not too long for a real child, the world of simple Nature being to him a wonderful, busy place through whose little dangers and pleasures he must pass his novitiate, and where his fresh mind finds a separate marvel in every experience. His eager fancy creates beauties out of the humblest things. The child's habit of living, as Emerson says of the poets, should be set on a key so low and plain that the common influences should delight him.[2] But our age of progress has perhaps wrought the child no greater evil than to raise him from this key to a lofty and most wretched falsetto; where, missing the early influences of Nature, and craving henceforth the taste for novelty he drew in with his milk, he has already exhausted life before the down is on his lip, and is worn out before he is in his teens.

In no direction is the taste and ingenuity of the world more busily employed than in designing and making toys. Here, grace of form and beauty of color are carefully contributed to furnish playthings for Nature's simplest creatures, her little children. But any thoughtful mother will tell you that such playthings do not amuse nearly as long as the ragdoll her little maiden made for her dimpled self, or the rough toy her boy fashioned from his own ever-restless energy. The world forgets that many of the toys most artistically

---

[2] From "The Poet" in *Essays, Second Series* (1844) by Ralph Waldo Emerson (1803-1882).

fashioned are designed from the grown person's standpoint, and though pleasing him as an exhibition of cunning mechanism, fail signally to interest the simple child.

Ruskin says in speaking of religious art, that "a rude symbol is often more effective than a refined one in touching the heart,"[3] a dogma that if questionable concerning grown people, is true beyond dispute in regard to children. A plaything that symbolizes something broadly is the noblest toy, since it leaves something for the child's fancy to complete, and is in no danger from its very finish of dwarfing his imagination. A doll of simple rude outline is a sketch, a hint, which the little girl's imagination may fill up with her tender young heart to draw upon, and which the beautiful effigy of waxen flesh, real hair, talking inside, with Parisian trousseau, complete and perfect, may fail to awaken.

Much of the indifference, ennui and discontent of our youth grows out of the finished splendor of their juvenile amusements, which satiating them early, leaves nothing for the future to equal or excel. Their baby hands are made to catch the octave stretch forlorn of our larger habits, and thus by our own training we develop them into all that is hard and artificial in our own adult selves, with an early contempt for the fair simplicities laid at their young feet by Nature, and a

---

[3] From *Modern Painters Vol. I,* Second Preface (1846) by John Ruskin (1819-1900), an English art critic and moralistic writer.

consequent irreverence that is simply appalling for all that concerns their elders.

In his ideal government of the "coming race," Bulwer[4] draws upon the good old past for one phase: he proposes a mingled aristocracy and democracy, which combination he reaches by making his grown-up people comprise the aristocracy, and his children the democracy. A most happy theory, if it bound the child to trust, reverence, obedience, and that blessed "audacity of faith" that would make him rest contentedly in the wisdom of a power on the earth greater than his puny self.

It was a thought in this direction that made Hazlitt[5] say, with epigrammatic truth, that the boy who did not think the Lord Mayor in his gilded coach[6] the greatest man in the world would live to be hung; and which was felt by Dr. Busby[7] on one occasion when King Charles II[8] paid his school a visit. The Doctor is said to have strutted through the school with his hat on, while his Majesty walked complacently behind him with hat under his arm. When he was taking leave, the Doctor said to the King: "I hope your Majesty will

---

[4] Sir Edward Bulwer-Lytton (1803-1873). A science fiction novelist who published *The Coming Race* (1871) about a utopian society.

[5] William Hazlitt (1778-1830). An English literary critic.

[6] Traditionally, the Lord Mayor of London rides in his "gilded coach" to the Royal Courts to pledge loyalty to the Crown.

[7] Dr. Richard Busby, headmaster of Westminster School in London from 1640-1695.

[8] King Charles II (1630-1685). Known for his easy-going nature.

excuse my want of respect hitherto, but if my boys were to imagine that there was a greater man in the kingdom than myself, I should never be able to rule them."

Go on, Science and Culture, and spin down the ringing grooves of change, but leave the children alone, spare them as Nature made them, and gain us once more a race of childish children, whom the spirit of iconoclasm, sacrilege and criticism has not reached, and to whom age is an honor that makes them somewhat shy, and beautifully timorous in the presence of their elders. Let our children once more be bade in the quaint old-fashioned words to "make their manners" before the grown folks, where ready honor shall be paid where honor is due. For where the minister is a saint, the schoolmaster a sovereign, and all the powers that be—from parents, through nurse, doctor, the mysterious lamplighter on his official rounds, the policeman with awful star on his breast, the "mayor in his gilded coach," up, up, to the highest dignitary in the land—where these exist in the child's obedient thoughts along with the genii and sultans and kings of his "Arabian Nights,"[9] we may borrow power from the child's fancy, and might from his obedience, and thus stamp upon his seal forever the beauty of law and the habit of reverence.

HUNTSVILLE, ALA.   [24 October 1877]   FLAKE WHITE

---

[9]   The classic collection of eastern tales such as "Ali Baba," "Sinbad the Sailor" and "Aladdin." Translated by E. W. Lane in 1840.

The Presbyterian Church of Huntsville in 1866 when Howard Weeden joined. The steeple was destroyed in a storm in 1876. Now known as the First Presbyterian Church, it is located at the corner of Gates Avenue and Lincoln Street, one block from The Weeden House.

Image from *History of The First Presbyterian Church, Huntsville, Alabama: Sesquicentennial Observance 1818-1968*; Charlotte and Donald Shenk; Paragon Press 1968.

LOW AND LOVELY SONGS

BY FLAKE WHITE

There are none of us who do not share in some degree Burrough's[1] wish to "migrate" when the spring comes. The beautiful earth is such a continual invitation to all that is bohemian in us; but after awhile the changing seasons lose their sweetness, and we turn sobered from the fading fields, conscious of a call upon another set of faculties than those in which we went a-maying. We leave the year to fold her azure tent, and turning indoors, we say

> 'Tis time to light the evening fire,
> To read good books, and sing
> The low and lovely songs that breathe
> Of the eternal spring.[2]

And we feel, with all who love these blessed songs, that no vivid world's spring, nor any poet or painter can ever render to the Christian heart

---

[1] John Burroughs (1837-1921). American naturalist and essayist.

[2] From "It's Time to Light the Evening Fires" by Alice Cary, American poet (1820-1871).

such a picture of the eternal spring as we find in the simplest hymn that chants the rapture of "Sweet fields arrayed in living green," and imparts such words as "I would not live always." In a burst of melody, we are reminded how the

> Rivers of pleasure flow o'er the bright plains,
> And the noontide of glory eternally reigns.[3]

Literary critics are wont to wonder why in a world of good poetry, its writers of hymns have so often clothed the grandest themes in mixed metaphors and doubtful rhymes. However this may be, the celestial themes hold immortal fire— and the most halting hymn, as well as the grandest, interprets the Christian heart, and burning through the dross of human words, bears us heavenward.

It would be very illuminating to know with what associations people at work or play absently hum such sacred airs as "Antioch," "Silver Street," "Dundee," "Old Hundred," and "Coronation"[4] —or softly breathe such words as "Rock of Ages,"[5] "Just as I Am,"[6] and "Jerusalem,

---

[3]   From the hymn "There is a Land of Pure Delight" (1707) by Isaac Watts (1674-1748).

[4]   Familiar tunes to which hymns are sung. For example: "Joy to the World" (Antioch); "Awake and Sing the Song" (Silver Street); "Our God, Our Help in Ages Past" (Dundee); "All People That on Earth Do Dwell" (Old Hundred); "All Hail the Power of Jesus' Name!" (Coronation).

[5]   "Rock of Ages"(1776) by Augustus M. Toplady (1740-1778).

My Happy Home."[7] You may be sure that they hold some tender message, earthly as well as heavenly.

Other songs, almost holy, may touch—but eternal songs touch and *hold*, and it is one of their deepest charms that we may fancy our dead as being reached by them, and perhaps, as still singing them!

So our hymns become our most faithful mementos. We may keep flowers and pictures, and tresses of hair—but the hymns that our dead once sung outlast them all. It was the human link they carried to heaven; it is the heavenly thing they left with us! We may have forgotten every song she[8] sung except a hymn. And yet, some day, in church or mart, the old words still wedded to the old tune merely fall upon our ear—and time suddenly drops away. Our beloved one is beside us once more, fresh and potent in the immortality of a hymn.

Those would be deaf ears that failed to catch the lullaby that breathes through old Nettleton's "Come, Thou Fount of Every Blessing,"[9] and not remember—as if it were yesterday—the mother's

---

[6] "Just as I Am" (1836) by Charlotte Elliott (1789-1871).

[7] "Jerusalem, My Happy Home" (1853) by Joseph Bromehead (1748-1826).

[8] Possibly a reference to Howard Weeden's mother, Jane Weeden, who died January 22, 1881.

[9] "Come, Thou Fount of Every Blessing" (1758) by Robert Robinson (1735-1790) sung to the tune of Nettleton.

bosom on which our young head cradled. The sense of rest and safety we felt in her warm, clasping arms still mixes with the heavenly words, and gives them an ineffable sweetness that makes this hymn an everlasting chant of peace.

As we grow older and encounter the strong and bitter creeds of life, we all have to unlearn some beautiful childish myths. But few of us will unlearn the precious theology from our early hymns, when our souls drank the truths—once and forever—in an elixir of song. When in a childish treble, we sang at our mothers' knees

> There is a happy land,
> Far, far away.[10]

Where we did not try to fathom, and though we have since then drifted about in a confusion of theories about Heaven, we still thank God in our best moments, returning to our childish creed caught in the melody of that hymn—when, lifting our eyes past our mother's face, we looked into the blue of the sky, and knew it was *There.*

Thank God for the church's hymns which have fed every age with riches till they girdle the world with a belt of song, sweet with the voices of children, deep with the cry of sinners, fragrant with the breath of saints, and purple with the blood of martyrs who have marched on to heaven, shouting their hallelujahs.

[6 February 1884]

---

[10] "There is a Happy Land," 1838, Andrew Young (1807-1889).

Sunday, June 28th, 1885, 3:30 p. m., at Presbyterian Church.

BIBLE AND SONG SERVICE.

Isa. i. 18; lv. I; Rev. xxii, 17.
To whom addressed.
Sinners. Isa. i, 18; Luke v, 32.
"Everyone that thirsteth " Isa. lv 1.
Gospel Hymns No. 127;
"He that hath no money." Isa. lv, 1.
The "heavy laden." Matt. ii, 28.
"Whosoever will." Rev. xxii, 17.
G. H. No. 10, 1, 2 verses.
When to be accepted.
"Come now." Isa. i, 18.
"Now is the accepted time." 2 Cor. vi, 2.
G H. No. 55; 1, 2 verses.
The result of accepting.
Purity. Isa, i, 18.
Satisfaction. Isa. lv, 1, 2
G. H. No. 169.
Rest. Matt. xi, 28.
G. H. No. 94.
Everlasting life. Rev. xxii, 17.
"Will in no wise cast out." John vi, 37.
G. H. No. 54; 1, 2, 5 verses.

From The Huntsville Weekly *Mercury*, June 24, 1885

Presbyterian Bible and Song Service
For Sunday, June 28, 1885

94

1 COME, thou Fount of every blessing,
Tune my heart to sing thy grace;
Streams of mercy, never ceasing,
Call for songs of loudest praise.

2 Teach me some melodious sonnet,
Sung by flaming tongues above;
Praise the mount! I'm fixed upon it,
Mount of God's unchanging love!

3 Here I raise my Ebenezer;
Hither by thy help I'm come;
And I hope, by thy good pleasure,
Safely to arrive at home.

4 Jesus sought me when a stranger,
Wandering from the fold of God;
He, to rescue me from danger,
Interposed his precious blood.

5 Oh, to grace how great a debtor
Daily I'm constrained to be!
Let that grace now, like a fetter,
Bind my wandering heart to thee.

6 Prone to wander, Lord, I feel it;
Prone to leave the God I love;
Here's my heart; oh, take and seal it,—
Seal it for thy courts above!

From *The Presbyterian Hymnal*, Philadelphia: Presbyterian Board of Publication, 1874

Hymn 94
"Come, Thou Fount of Every Blessing"

REV. SAM JONES AT HUNTSVILLE
LETTER TO A D.D.

My Dear Doctor[1] —Yes, I got your letter telling me not to write you any more rhapsodies about the Rev. Sam Jones, the revivalist;[2] that when you wanted theology you preferred taking it out of deep old wells (with a Greek bucket and a Hebrew windlass[3])! Of course I know that, and how scholarly your defense of a learned clergy always is—but when you hear that almost every friend you have in Huntsville has come to Christ through this man, I know you will want to know something of his way—a way that is absolutely apostolic in its simplicity.

---

[1]   Howard Weeden responds to any "learned" critic of Sam Jones by writing a "letter to a D. D." who is a "Doctor of Divinity."

[2]   Samuel Porter Jones (1847-1906). An evangelist born in Alabama and reared in Georgia who attracted national attention for preaching a simple gospel message. In 1885, Jones preached in Huntsville for eight days, four times daily, to overflowing crowds at the Methodist Church. (See "The Religious Cyclone," Huntsville Weekly *Independent*, 12 February 1885:3.)

[3]   Windlass. A hand-operated machine used to hoist a heavy object.

Did you ever think what strange use religious economy makes of simple preachers? How once or more in every age the heavy, incense-laden air, through which the priestly voices sound faint and far off, is broken by a rush as of wings, and sudden room is made for a new John the Baptist,[4] with the freshness of the wilderness upon him, or for a Peter the Hermit[5] in worn sandals leading a new crusade with "race dust on his cheek"!

The world always credits a miraculous power to such men; there is a conspicuous absence of contemporary fashions and flavor of learning, and the tricks of schools that make their utterances sound like the words of God. For all their electricity, these reformers are periodic, and the world receives them as if it had been waiting. When Mr. Jones (I wish his name was Thomas Aquinas,[6] for your sake!) came to us last week, there seemed a silence in the air, then there was a keen note from a not "uncertain" trumpet, and all at once we were at his feet.

Uncertain? Why, from the moment he enters the pulpit and begins the simple service, there is an unhesitating straightforwardness, as if the act itself was the law of God. It seems foreordained!

---

4   John the Baptist. The New Testament prophet who announced the Lord's coming and preached repentance (Matthew 3:1-6).

5   Peter the Hermit (c.1050-1115). A French ascetic preacher, considered one of the early leaders of the First Crusade.

6   Thomas Aquinas (c.1225-1274). A scholastic theologian and philosopher who used reason to explain doctrines of faith.

After noting that he is small, slight and dark, a face of which one only remembers purpose and expression, one takes a note of settled courage. He is so small, so mere a speck as he glances over the sea of faces greeting him, that with a look of quiet welcome and possession he changes suddenly into a magnet, from which his audience never again escapes. His voice is a powerful factor; it is even, temperate, and at first slightly monotonous, like one who is delivering a message from an unseen voice at his ear.

Suddenly the man who has quietly thrilled you is making you laugh, and some roughs in the corner over there are applauding—and when you leave him a few minutes later, they and you are weeping. How can you help either the laughter or the tears? He makes our apostasy so sad, and Heaven so sweet; and he tells the story so simply, enriching it with similes so broad and homely that our humanness bubbles over with pleasure. The farmer, the merchant, the fisherman, the little child are all used as illustrations. It is the old parable preaching: the sower, the prodigal son, the good Samaritan, the lost sheep! We are knit into the theme by the common incidents of daily life, until the air is soft with human sweetness; then suddenly he lifts his slight arm like a cleaving wing, and heaven opens, and we shade our eyes from the light, as he tells us in panting words of its glory—in words that are still not learned or elegant, but fly from him in sparks as if beaten from some molten mass by an unseen hand!

You remember old Martin, who has been to the coal mines so frequently—he says, as the tears stream down his dark face, that "Mr. Jones has got sympathy for folks," which is in truth about half the matter.

I know a Bishop who always sends his young preachers to read George Eliot's sketch of the woman-preacher, Dinah Morris.[7] It's well to read it, but it can't be copied. The charm and power of Dinah is her womanly pity, her divine humanness. Mr. Jones loves, pities sinners—pleads for them on his knees, and to them on his feet—and his sweet compassion, like a warm Gulf Stream, melts them from their icy anchors and floats them past the tide of mortal, to the sea of heavenly love.

Surely the poet might have said that not only "he prayeth best who loveth best,"[8] but he preacheth best who loveth best.

Yours truly,
FLAKE WHITE

Huntsville, Ala., February 9, 1885

---

[7] A character in the novel *Adam Bede* (1859) by George Eliot (pseudonym for Mary Ann Evans, 1819-1880).

[8] From "The Rime of the Ancient Mariner" (1797) by Samuel Taylor Coleridge (1772-1834).

Image courtesy of Rose Lawn Museum

Samuel Porter Jones (1847-1906)

Editorial Note

"Rev. Sam Jones at Huntsville" was originally published in the *Christian Observer*, February 18, 1885, and reprinted in the Huntsville *Independent*, February 26, 1885, with the *Independent's* note:

> The following letter signed "Flake White" dated "Huntsville, Ala.; February 9, 1885," is too well-written to be withheld from our readers. It is said to have been written by a fair hand whose pen is evidently as clever as her pencil is skillful.

Image courtesy of Phillips Auctioneers, Ltd.

"Birch Forest in Winter" by Carl Brenner (1838-1888)

The work of Carl Brenner, a well-known landscape artist, was represented at the Nashville Art Exhibition.

Editorial Note

The following letter to the Huntsville *Independent* about the Art Exhibition in Nashville was composed during the time that Howard Weeden was writing as "Flake White" and was signed simply "W." Her visit to Nashville for this event was documented in the Nashville *Union* and reprinted in the Huntsville *Mercury* on April 30, 1885:

> Miss Howard Weeden, of Huntsville, is in the city, a guest of Dr. Price. Miss Weeden is an artist of some reputation, and has several water colors on exhibition here that indicate merit of no common order. Her works are very much admired. —Nashville *Union*

NASHVILLE ART EXPOSITION

*D*ear *Editor Independent:*

To those who have been hoping that the development of Southern Industries would someday give us the Arts also—when we might hear Music through the roar of her furnaces and see Pictures through the smoke of her factories— the success of the recent Art Exposition at Nashville has been a subject of hearty congratulation.

We went to it pledged to be pleased with so noble a purpose, but prepared to pardon a thousand shortcomings incident to so young an enterprise; we found it a ripe, rich feast of Art, with nothing to forgive and everything to praise.

It was with a feeling of no small surprise that we spent our first evening at the New Exhibition and noted the charming composure with which Nashville had accepted her first brilliant success. The beautiful gallery was brilliantly lighted and flooded with music from an Italian band hidden in some imagined nook, as if playing in their native land! The walls glowed everywhere with pictures, and a throng of art-loving, soft-voiced people (as if they were of Italy, too) moved along the ample floors, with worshipful eyes uplifted or studiously bent upon annotated catalogues, while artistic repartee mingled with pleasant laughter, or classic chatter from groups of Vanderbilt students, where Dr. Worman[1] or Dr. Price[2] held momentary tournaments—made a scene "cultured" enough to have seemed Boston, had it not already seemed—Italy! A glance at the terra cotta-bound catalogue, compiled by Mr. Theo. Cooley[3]—whose deeds for the enterprise in a thousand generous ways would make another catalogue—had already given a list of well known, famous loans: Peace's "John the Baptist"; Rierstadt's "Among the Clouds"; Bristol's "Mt. Chocorua"; De Haas's "Fresh Breeze"; Montgcazza's "Marriage in the Park," and many

---

[1]   Dr. James Worman, professor at Vanderbilt University 1883-1886.

[2]   Dr. George W. F. Price (1830-1899), a lifelong friend of Howard Weeden, was the President of Tuskegee Female College where she studied during the Civil War. Subsequently, he and his family moved to Huntsville where he served as President of the Huntsville Female College until 1880, then moved to Tennessee to establish the Nashville College for Young Ladies. His daughter, Elizabeth Fraser Price, was a devoted friend to Howard Weeden.

[3]   Theodore Cooley, formerly of Huntsville, was the recipient of Howard Weeden's own contributions to the Nashville Art Exhibit (as noted in the Huntsville *Independent*, 5 March 1885:3).

others, to which visitors brought a ready recognition.

A thousand lovers of Carl Brenner[4] stood beneath his "Beech Trees" and fondly wished they might cut his—the name all Nashville loves—upon their silvery trunks.

A score of masterful pictures from Miss May, of Memphis, made one wonder if *her* camel's-hair brush was not lion's-hair!

The Vedder[5] designs were in themselves an Exposition, and would require, as they will no doubt receive from learned voice and pen in Nashville, a discriminating review.

The Exposition was financially a great success, the results paying expenses and leaving a generous sum with which to purchase many of the best loans to remain permanently on the Gallery walls; besides a liberal patronage from citizens who purchased largely of the pictures to add, in future, new grace to Nashville's already cultivated homes.

W.

April 29, 1885

---

[4]   Carl Brenner (1838-1888) resided in Louisville, KY. As a landscape artist, he frequently painted the beech woods of Kentucky.

[5]   Elihu Vedder (1836-1923). An American artist known for allegorical and landscape paintings.

Moody and Sankey at Selma, Ala.

Dwight L. Moody (1837-1899)

Editorial Note

Howard Weeden wrote "Moody and Sankey at Selma, Ala." while she was visiting her brother, Dr. Henry V. Weeden of Dallas County. (Huntsville *Independent*, 11 March 1886:3; 15 April 1886:3.) Her article was first published in the *Christian Observer* March 24, 1886. The Huntsville *Independent* reprinted the article on April 1, 1886 with the following note:

> The letter of Flake White which we reproduce is written in her best, most charming mood. Her letters are always read with eager pleasure.

Moody And Sankey

AT SELMA, ALA.

It is probably that no one ever passed through a Moody and Sankey[1] meeting without an effort to send an account of it to some less favored person, only to become so baffled by the elusive character of Mr. Moody as to be tempted to evade all analysis of him, and take refuge in a description of Mr. Sankey's singing, and in statistics of the crowds that came to hear them.

The recent meeting that opened at Selma last Sunday afternoon was no exception to the rule. Indeed, the strange character of the local "scenery" prepared for the occasion; it dislocated all one's previous ideas of a religious meeting and left no faculty at work, except the imagination. The place selected was a cotton warehouse,

---

[1] Dwight L. Moody (1837-1899). A successful Christian evangelist who travelled world-wide holding revivals. He was accompanied by the organist and singer, Ira D. Sankey (1840-1908).

stretching its low length across an entire block, along whose uneven floor lay a bewildering vista of rough benches; overhead, a maze of bare rafters spanned the ceiling, and through them the sun lighted unevenly the monotony of the long, low brick walls.

When Mr. Moody rose in his simple rostrum, there seemed an immediate adjustment of proprieties. The vast, unadorned place could not have better suited the large, unaffected man; for it was no slender David with a sling[2] that appeared, but a giant, a gladiator; and when he delivered his message, it was no "smooth stone" that he threw; it was a cloud-burst, a roar of many waters, under which one sat in a sort of terror, till collected senses began presently to catch through the storm such words as Love, Heaven, Redemption, Peace—and the Light, slowly bursting through the rain, made prisms of the words—as one sat in a glowing bow of Promise.

If one could choose from among the complexity of mental riches Mr. Moody offers as a speaker, it would probably be his supreme gift as a sacred biographer—the vivid power with which he restores to our small faith and meagre fancy the remote lives that people God's word.

We have in him, once more, the vanished "storyteller," who flourished before the age of books, who in palace or tent, in the pause of

---

[2] David, the young shepherd boy who slew Goliath (1 Samuel 17).

battle or the ennui of peace, restored the lives of past heroes, and made to his listeners future heroism possible.

He narrates simply without poetic license or trick of rhetoric; but he is deep, in earnest; he is a gladiator in body, and a hero in heart. He has lived on the great earnest lives of God's past people, till they have entered his soul and filled his veins with their deep, red blood, and quickened his pulses with their fierce heartbeats. He leads us to the dawn of time, and behind the flood shows us Noah, and through the spray of the Red Sea gives us Moses.[3] He tells us of Job and Jonah[4] till they cease to seem sacred fables; he takes John and Peter, and such slight sketches as Joseph of Arimathea, Nicodemus, Herod and Pilate,[5] and transforms them suddenly into a series of finished frescoes—foreshortened till we stand beside them, and feel their breath upon our cheek.

He takes us across the centuries and makes us walk with these men, and wherever we start, and by whatever road we go, we always come at

---

[3] Moody portrays the Creation (Genesis 1), the Flood (Genesis 6-9), and the Exodus (Exodus 14:13-31).

[4] Men who were dramatically humbled by their God.

[5] People who played important roles in the story of Jesus: John and Peter became key apostles to Jesus (Mark 3:16-17); Joseph of Arimathea entombed Jesus (Matthew 27:57-60); Nicodemus, a religious teacher, learned from Jesus (John 3:1-21); Herod and Pilate authorized the crucifixion of Jesus (Luke 23:1-25).

last to Calvary.[6] From Adam to John, from Eve to Mary[7] we stay our weary feet finally at the Cross,[8] and hear always the peroration of these stories in the light of the Transfiguration.[9]

It is from Mr. Moody that we have gotten, at last, the real New Version—in one syllable[10] and heaven's idiom.

He has renewed human kinship with the Bible race, till he has re-created our past as well as illumined our future, and taught us with new faith that all the graves that lie between cannot break the crimson thread[11] that binds us to the Adam of the Old Testament and the Lord of the New.

SELMA, ALA.   FLAKE WHITE
[24 March 1886]

---

[6]   The place where Jesus was crucified (Mark 15:22-24).

[7]   From the books of Genesis to Revelation: from the mother of mankind (Genesis 3:20) to the mother of God's Son (Luke 1:31-33).

[8]   At the cross where Jesus' death atoned for the sins of the world (Colossians 1:19-20).

[9]   When the face of Jesus "shone like the sun and his clothes became as white as light" (Matthew 17:1-3).

[10]   Possibly, love. "God is love" (1 John 4:8-10).

[11]   The blood of the eternal covenant (Hebrews 13:20).

THE WORK IN EGYPT

BY FLAKE WHITE

Dear Observer—Your correspondent had the pleasure, a few days since, of seeing a foreign souvenir which if measured by artistic standard alone would make it of matchless value. It is an Egyptian coffee service, consisting of a lovely dark red pitcher (which does duty instead of our ugly coffeepot) and a cup and vase, accompanied by a card inscribed in Arabic, a beautiful tangle of characters more like an embroidered wreath than writing and not unlike that which ornaments the pitcher—as if to show that whether an Egyptian makes a coffeepot or writes a line, he must do it alike: majestically.

They are made from the Nile mud, and could they speak, what would they not say of that wondrous river that flows along the Pyramids that knew the Pharaohs and that cradled Moses!

The service was a parting gift, a benediction, from our young missionary, Miss Isabella Strang,[1]

---

[1] Daughter of David Strang (1836-1917) who served as a missionary to Egypt in the early 1870's and later as a minister of the Presbyterian church in Lincoln, Tennessee.

who after a few months' rest in her native country, is now returning to Egypt, the land of her sacred exile! During her vacation she visited Huntsville, a guest of Mrs. McCracken,[2] and those who had the privilege of hearing her talks about that wonderful country will not soon forget them. She has lived there since childhood so that it seems like a native land, and her talks are so simple and unpremeditated that one wonders how her unadorned descriptions can so give the light and color of that splendid old world. But the very words she scatters along her low-voiced talks carry a grave splendor in themselves, and she does not need to affect eloquence who has at her service such words as Alexandria, Cairo, the Nile, the Sphinx, the Pyramids, and can at will chant a commandment in solemn Arabic, or softly sing a psalm in the same language!

Against this historic background she paints the modern aspect of the Church as it now exists in Egypt where it is kept alive by such earnest workers as herself, by struggling converts, and by humble Copts,[3] who represent the Faith, as against the stately old Mohammedan who still sits with his red-bound Koran,[4] the changeless image of Law and Tradition.

It is likely the writer will never forget a devotional service that followed one of Miss Strang's lectures here, when chancing to sit

---

[2]   The J. L. McCrackens of the Presbyterian church in Huntsville.

[3]   Christians who are native Egyptians.

[4]   The sacred book of the Islamic faith.

beside her we sang from the same book. The hymn chosen happened to be that gospel jubilate, "We'll work till Jesus comes."[5] All at once, the claim to be working for Him seemed on our part to be a great presumption in comparison with this missionary, who, in so grand a sense, has truly gone about her "Father's business."

She is accompanied this trip by a younger sister who joins her in the sacred work. The two have thus left all to follow Him, and are henceforth affectionately commended to Heaven's care and keeping.

HUNTSVILLE, ALA
[8 September 1886]

---

[5]   "We'll Work Till Jesus Comes," by Elizabeth Mills (1805-1829).

The Old Folk's Concert

Image from the Huntsville Weekly *Democrat*, 18 February 1903.

Editorial Note

In a letter to her friend, Elizabeth Price,[1] Howard Weeden mentions having attended and written about the Old Folk's Concert:

> I spent a pleasant evening not long since at Mrs. Oliver Patton's in attending the old folks concert . . . . I put up a paper to send you days ago containing a copy of a little notice I wrote of it, but it failed to go, so I send it now.[2]

[1] Elizabeth Price, a prominent musician of Nashville, was an ardent friend and promoter of Howard Weeden's artwork. (See Fisk and Roberts, *Shadows on the Wall: The Life and Works of Howard Weeden*, 21-22.)

[2] Howard Weeden to Elizabeth Price, February or March 1895. Howard Weeden Collection (Huntsville-Madison County Public Library).

For the Huntsville Weekly *Argus*

THE OLD FOLK'S CONCERT

Old loves, old aspirations and old dreams,
More beautiful for being old and gone!

All the world went Monday evening to the Old Folk's Concert at Mr. Oliver Patton's[1] and was reminded afresh of the fine things the author of *Trilby*[2] has been telling us lately about the charms and powers of music.

How we wish du Maurier had been there and poetic Little Billie whose heart used to bleed so profusely whenever he heard "Alice, Ben Bolt!"[3] It would not have bled only, but have broken altogether, at hearing "Long Ago," and "Come Sang Awa," and "Rosin the Beau," and "Auld Lang Syne"[4] and all the other old, old songs through

---

[1] Oliver Beirne Patton (1848-1909) and his wife, Elizabeth Irvine White (1847-1918), lived at 417 McClung Avenue.

[2] *Trilby* (1894), a novel by George du Maurier, about a young girl whose engagement to Little Billie ends when she is taken away by a Hungarian musician. Under his influence she becomes a great singer, but dies an untimely death.

[3] "Don't you remember sweet Alice, Ben Bolt," (1843) a song by Thomas Dunn English about love and separation.

[4] "Auld Lang Syne,"(1788) attributed to Robert Burns (1756-1796). A song about olden times.

whose simple airs one seemed to feel the heartbeat of a century of singers who had loved, and sung and passed away.

How Little Billie's artistic eye would have feasted upon the lovely candle-lit room, soft in the "light of other days," and its groups of quaint singers in their caps and kerchiefs and powdered hair, looking more like a collection of mellow miniatures than real personages!

What heirlooms they wore! Wedding gowns and lockets and laces, smelling of lavender and memories till one felt all the loved and lost of a lifetime come back and greet one through a mist of tears!

And how Little Billie would have enjoyed the handshaking after the Doxology;[5] and with what a high-bred air he would have asked to kiss Aunt Ruthy's[6] cheek; and how much better than any of the rest of us, he would have found happy words in which to thank one lovely hostess for our delightful evening.

[17 January 1895]   H. W.

---

[5]   Doxology. A hymn beginning with "Praise God from who all blessings flow."

[6]   Aunt Ruth Partington. A comic figure of the mid-1800's known for her malapropisms; created by Ben Shillaber. Appearing as "Aunt Ruthy" at the concert was Mrs. Virginia Clay-Clopton, former wife of Alabama Senator Clement Claiborne Clay (see "Ye Olde Folkes," Huntsvillle Weekly *Democrat*, 17 January 1895:3). In her memoirs, Mrs. Clay-Clopton describes her celebrated impersonation of "Aunt Ruthy" at a ball in Washington D. C. (*A Belle of the Fifties*. New York: Doubleday, 1904. Chapter IX.)

Anton Rubinstein (1829-1894)

For the Huntsville Weekly *Democrat*[1]

ANTON RUBINSTEIN

Anton Gregore Rubinstein was born at Wechwotyuetz on November 28th, 1829. He had the happiness of having his mother as his first teacher in music, but at the age of eleven years, was already such a prodigy that he was taken to Paris to study and there, among other advantages, had the good fortune to meet the famous Listz.[2]

In 1842 we find him in London playing before the then young and lovely Queen,[3] and from that time until his death, November 29, 1894, his musical recitals throughout the world were a succession of unparalleled triumphs.

When one takes up his pen to write of Rubinstein, he is reminded of what Victor Hugo[4]

---

[1]   Weeden wrote this characterization for the Music Literary Club which met in the home of Captain Milton Humes, July 16, 1895.

[2]   Franz Listz (1811-1886). A Hungarian pianist and composer.

[3]   Queen Victoria of England who reigned from 1837-1901.

[4]   Victor Hugo (1802-1885). A French poet, novelist and dramatist.

says somewhere of a great character: that it stood like a "name written in the snow by the finger of a giant."

Everything about him was large: his country was the vast Russias, across the snows of whose unmeasured steppes there was room to write Rubinstein.

His church was the majestic Catholic, crowded with splendid votaries, but with room for Rubinstein.

His race was the imperishable Hebrew—reaching back to the flood—with its poets, prophets, priests and kings, and yet with room for Rubinstein!

It is no wonder that such imperial sources, pouring their riches into his nature, made him so broad that common words do not seem to describe him fitly. Certainly a history of his music alone is not sufficient. His biographer would have had something to say had the robust Rubinstein not played a note. His fingers did not drain his mind, for he was a philosopher, and scholar; nor did they drain his heart, for he was princely in his charities, and devoted in his friendships.

It is to the lasting honor of the Czar[5] that he was Rubinstein's unalterable friend and patron, and when Time shall have dimmed the Autocrat's glories till they are scarcely remembered, it will still be told of this Czar that when he died, one man's heart broke for grief and that great heart was Rubinstein's!

[24 July 1895]   HOWARD WEEDEN

---

[5]   Alexander II Romanov (1855-1881). Founded the St. Petersburg conservatory with Anton Rubinstein as director.

Stories

View of the Church of the Nativity from an
upstairs bedroom of The Weeden House

PATIENCE

It was a bright day in September—the first of the new session—and the boys looked with longing eyes at the ripening nuts in the woods, and on the partridges that, already beginning to whistle under the hedges, promised such fine sport.

"I wish this was the last day of school instead of the first," said Charles Merrill, a bright, intelligent boy, who stood leaning against the schoolhouse door. "I hate to think the pleasant days have all gone."

"I do, too, but we will just have to make the best of the present, and wait with patience for another summer."

"Well-spoken," said Mr. Olin, the master, as he joined the group clustered round the door and laid his hand on the shoulder of the last speaker—a small, pale boy, whose stick (his constant companion) and halting walk proclaimed him one of God's chastened ones. "Well-spoken. Patience is a great virtue."

A few minutes after, the bell called the scholars into the long-deserted schoolroom.

"I hope, my dear boys," said the master, "that you have had a pleasant holiday. I should like to hear you tell of what you have seen through this long, bright summer. I have seen some pleasant things, too, and the remark I made just before school reminds me of an incident that I think will interest you. In travelling several weeks ago among the mountains, whose distant peaks you can just see from the hill, I stopped to enjoy the view below me when an unusual sound reached my ear.

"It was the voice of one singing a sweet song. I could hear no words, but the tune sounded as if it were accustomed to singing God's praise. I turned and followed the sound until I stopped before a low rude house, dark with age and gloomy under the shade the black cedars threw upon it.

"The music ceased when I knocked, and a pleasant voice said, 'Come in.' I opened the door and was about to ask a question concerning my road when the appearance of my host compelled me to enter. He was an old man with white hair and a bent figure, coarsely but neatly clad. He was rising to give me the only chair in the room, but, begging him to be seated, I leaned against the old brown stone chimney and watched him with interest as he sunk back into the chair, wearied with the slight effort of rising.

'I am a feeble old man,' he said.

'Do you live here alone?' I asked.

'Yes,' he replied, 'Except for the few travellers who pass, I see no one. Thirty years ago,' he continued, 'I built this house. I was a stonecutter and earned a good living, but in lifting a great rock I received an injury, and for twenty years I've hardly left this house.'

'Are you often lonely?' I asked.

'I used to be,' he said, 'for friends forget me, and travellers rarely notice me—but,' he added cheerfully, 'I have learned not to run with patience the race set before me, but to do what is harder, *to stand and wait patiently.*'

'How do you spend your time?' I inquired after a pause.

"He drew towards him an old box, and from among a few tools took out several roughly carved pieces—a cross or two, an anchor, and a vase.

'This is all I can do,' he said meekly, 'and my old trembling fingers worked on them many weeks.'

"He again took from the box a cloth, which he unwrapped, and drew forth a small image.

'I have just finished it,' he went on; 'it has taken a year, but it is the figure of Patience, and I loved working upon it.' "

Mr. Olin paused, and took from the desk the figure of an old man bending under a huge cross with his eyes raised hopefully and his hands clasped calmly and meekly. It was roughly but ingeniously carved.

"I bought it, thanking God for the lesson the old man had taught me," said Mr. Olin. "Now, boys," he continued, "I want to make you a proposition. A year from now I will give this figure of Patience to the boy who has given most evidence of growth in the beautiful virtue which it teaches."

That evening as they were leaving the schoolyard, Charles Merrill arrested the steps of the boys with the proposition to go over and get some of old Isaac's apples while he was gone to the mill.

"It would be downright stealing," indignantly said Paul Gray, the lame boy.

"I'd like to see you climb after them, Cripple," sneered one of the boys.

The hot blood mounted into the lame boy's face and, turning away, he left the playground to go and throw himself on the grass at home and sob out, "Oh—why was I made the jest and laughing stock of the world!" But suddenly the memory of his teacher's story rose in his mind, and he said—"Well, I suppose this is my cross, and I must bear it if I ever hope for reward."

It was many months after. The ground was white with snow, and the boys were flocking to school. Snowballs were flying like leaves in the fall. Charles Merrill was just entering the schoolyard gate when a ball loaded with ice sped through the air and sent him reeling to the ground.

"Where did that come from?" he shouted, jumping up, while the playground rung with laughter. Seeing a boy behind a nearby tree, Charles started toward him.

"It wasn't me," cried Paul Gray, trying to stifle his laughter.

"It was, sir," said Charles, and dealt a blow that felled him to the ground.

Paul was not severely hurt and rose as the boys gathered around. "You were mistaken, Charles," he said, quietly brushing the snow from his clothes and entering the school just as Mr. Olin left the window from which he had witnessed the deed. It had cost Paul a great effort not to return the blow, but the image of Patience with the Cross had been stronger than pride, and had conquered.

The year was past. The nuts were ripening again in the woods. The boys were all gathered in the schoolroom, and Mr. Olin stood with Patience before him.

"My dear friends," he said, "many of you have no doubt forgotten the proposition I made a year ago. Some of you have not, I know, for I have watched you, and am gratified at the worthy manner in which you have conquered a want of perseverance in your studies. One of you I have noticed with much interest. He has proved himself mightier than he who taketh a city—he has ruled his own spirit. I award to Paul Gray the image. Do you agree with me, boys?"

They paused a moment and, as they thought over the many reproaches patiently borne, there went up a universal "Yes!" and no voice was heartier than Charles Merrill's. Mr. Olin carried the image to Paul, and laying his hand on his head, said, "May God bless you and grant that, having lived as patiently as the old man whom I saw for the last time the other day, you may die as peacefully."

[8 February 1866]   FLAKE WHITE

THE OLD PICTURE

Among a number of pictures in a certain ancient gallery—collected there by an old man, long, long since dead—there hangs a little piece of embroidery. One wonders to find this moth-eaten cloth amidst the rich display of rare canvasses and carved frames that surround it. Though it bears only a simple design of flowers and thorns in faded colors, it still retains a grace that decay has not removed, and a tenderness that time can not destroy. You would not pass it carelessly by, even to see the magnificence beyond, if you but knew its little story, "simple as nature, sorrowful as life."

Its owner was a man of great wealth, and being alone in the world, spent it with fabulous prodigality upon pictures, a rare collection of which he was amassing. He seemed to have "thrust canvas" between himself and humanity, for so indifferent was he, that neither his gold nor kind words ever went to heal the sorrows of others.

One of his favorite rambles through the quaint old city in which he lived lay along a narrow, crooked street, all ruinous and dark with crumbling houses on either side, whose gloom and poverty were in marked contrast to the richness of his own dress.

In passing near a decaying tenement one evening, he noticed that a low window, long closed and choked with dust, was now open. Glancing in, he saw a girl, pale and poorly clad. She bent earnestly over some work, her face serious yet free from discontent, so profoundly and beautifully patient, that he remembered it long after he had passed. When he looked for her the next evening, he found the patient worker still there just as before, only more pale and weary. When he saw the lonely and cheerless room, he marvelled at her peaceful face.

So the gentle face in the window began to have an interest for the old man; how great he did not know until one evening he found the shutter closed. Pausing abruptly as if missing something, he turned to a child who sat on the low doorstep, and asked her, pointing to the window, "Who lived in there?"

"Only Poor Agnes," said the child, shaking her head, "that's all we call her and all we know about her, except that she is very good. She is sick now." The child drew her little hand across her tearful eyes while the old man went slowly on his way.

Several days elapsed before he passed that way again, and found the window once more open. Pausing this time to look in, he perceived that the girl was working upon a piece of embroidery into which her thin fingers were slowly weaving the gay threads that seemed to have stolen all the brightness from her face, so wan and colorless did it look. Her design was simply a crown of thorns woven about with a wreath of passionflowers. The cruel sharpness of the thorns was rendered with wonderful truthfulness, and the grace and richness of the flowers with such depth of tenderness. He gazed upon the emblem in astonishment. Presently through the window, he asked, "Why have you worked thorns and passionflowers together?"

She looked up with a start at the sound of his voice, then turning back to her picture, spoke thoughtfully. "They seem to come naturally together. The story of these thorns is Bible truth, you know. They were man's reward to our Lord for His life of suffering and holiness. He wore these thorns so that a crown of glory might be secured for us hereafter; he bore them as an example of the suffering that none of us can escape."

"These flowers," Agnes continued, touching the half-withered ones in her lap, "tradition tells us are holy, too. They never grew, it is said, until our Saviour's agony in the garden, when they then and there sprung up, a prophecy of His death to come." Pointing to her passionflowers, she said, "See the purple robe of scorn, the drops of blood, the crown of thorns, the nails and hammer! It is a long and awful story to be written in so small a flower. So both have become precious symbols to me, the thorns, of His world-witnessed martyrdom; and the flowers, of that lonely agony that none saw but God. Christ knew that many of us would not suffer in sight of the multitude and would have to wrestle alone."

A new wonderment, followed by a strange softness came into the listener's face. After a little pause, he told Agnes that he wished to purchase her work when finished. The wondrous story had touched the old man, and moved his heart unwontedly as the days passed while he waited for Agnes.

In the meantime, the man's interest in her picture had stirred new energies in poor desolate Agnes. Rousing herself, she worked earnestly upon it, unconscious that she was weaving another mournful story into her symbol of revered history. At last, one evening she put a final stitch into it, and laying aside the bunch of withered flowers, she sat gazing at her completed work until her weary head drooped over it and she fell asleep.

The old man, passing the window that evening, spoke to her but received no answer. Quietly he entered the little, lonely room that the sunlight was filling with strange shadows. He touched the bowed figure softly, but it did not stir. Poor Agnes' work was finished. Her young life of care, self-denial, patience and sorrow was over. But, its memory lived on after her.

Her work was hung by its new owner as chief among his pictures. He never wearied telling its story. Others touched by its recital still tell it after him to show how one sorrowful life and death was meekly pictured by another.

HUNTSVILLE, ALA.   F. W.
[18 June 1868]

"I have thought that wild flowers might be the alphabet of angels, whereby they write on hills and fields mysterious truths."—FRANCIS.

THE BLOSSOMING CROSS

I fashioned, one day, from a thorny bough
    A little slender cross,
Whose cruel thorns all clustered close,
    The old, old story told:
Uniting the grief of the grievous crown
    To the woe of the woeful cross.
And sinking its shaft in the mellow earth,
    At its feet a vine I planted,
That was green and tender and dream-like
       enough
    To have sprung from uncursed ground.
I twisted its delicate tendrils round
    The bare pathetic cross,
And watered daily with hopeful heart
    My beautiful dainty vine.
But alas! It drooped and faded away,
    Like earthly wishes fair,
And I bitterly asked, "Why was it denied?
    'Twas lovely, and therefore, good!"
The tears fell away from my blinded eyes
    And showed me a heavenly thing!
The vine had died, but the cross had budded,
    For every thorn a leaf!
And I cried in the joy born out of my grief,
    "Lord, what Thou doest is well!
The gifts Thy sternest wisdom decrees
    Exceed our fairest desires."

HUNTSVILLE, ALA.   [25 April 1877]   FLAKE WHITE

THE ROCK THAT IS HIGHER THAN I

Upon a small island, so cheerless in its monotony of ashen sand and gray rocks, and so barren in its scarcity of vegetation that it seemed a home fit only for the seabird, there once stood among its meagre collection of houses a small weather-beaten hut, that, notwithstanding its comfortless exterior, was the pleasant home of a fisherman, his wife and son.

The room in which the good wife was busied "upon household cares intent" was a model of the picturesque which would have pleased the fancy of a Flemish painter. The walls were black with the smoke a hundred wild winds had blown down the wide stone chimney, and served as a fine background for the drapery of sails, fishermen's coats, and nets that hung from it. The nets now all turned into golden meshes in the firelight that glowed on the ample hearth. Within its genial glow sat the fisherman drying his damp garments, and talking now and then of his day's labors. "Where is Gilbert?" he said suddenly. "It grows late."

"I hope," replied his wife, "that he has gone to John Lea's to see the man of God who is there preaching. I have begged him many times to go, but he always refused until this evening, when he almost promised."

"Gilbert is a hard lad," her husband said, with mingled sadness and tenderness. "He is so fearless of all that worldly things can do that he seems to feel no need of Heaven," and while he spoke the door opened and Gilbert, a boy about twelve years, entered.

"Well, Mother," he said, taking a seat near the fire. "I've been to see the preacher, and to hear him talk, one would think he was a sailor; he loves the sea as much as I do, and he says Christ loved it, too, for He walked along it, and upon it, and preached on it and by it, and that His disciples were fishermen. He says, too, that wise men in all ages have drawn morals from it, and that we who live by it ought to take its lessons to heart."

"Yes," said the father, shaking his head earnestly, "the sea is a great teacher. I remember when a boy, I was a wild fellow and often cruelly neglected my mother who was an invalid and alone in the world. One Sabbath evening she persuaded me to leave a sailing party and walk with her on the beach—and as we walked she talked of Heaven and those holy things that claimed so little of my attention. Then she placed one of her gathered shells by my childish ear and asked me what it said, while she held one by her own ear, gazing with a far-off look to the sea, that drew me toward her with a yearning I had never felt before, and made me wonder if she was looking into eternity. But surely as God spoke to Job out of the whirlwind, He spoke to me in the still and small voice of the shell, and I never hear one now but I remember the counsels she gave. Soon after," said the old man pausing a moment, "she left the earthly shell and went where only the pearls are."

The next day Gilbert and his father went in their little boat over to a neighboring island. Although the latter had not been deceived in the weather as it appeared early in the morning, he was hardly prepared for its rapid change toward noon and, anxious to get home before the storm should come in all its fury, he and Gilbert were soon embarked for home. The wind was roaring with prophetic rage, and as the boat made its fearful way, the air grew heavy with the advancing storm, and the flying sea gulls' wings gleamed white against the sky. As they neared a rocky cape of their island where the waves were churning themselves white and dashing foam into the pallid faces of the voyagers, a terrible roll of thunder seemed to shake the sea into greater fury and the boat—was gone.

The wave that threw the helpless boat into oblivion, and the "ancient mariner" into eternity, threw Gilbert upon the sand. For awhile, he lay stunned and bewildered, looking through the twilight at the crested waves, until he saw them each moment advancing upon his low retreat. Staggering to his feet, he shrieked wildly while the waters dashed higher and higher. As a wild prayer for mercy escaped his white lips he turned and saw at a little distance from him a tall rock—standing unshaken, when all else around it was convulsed—a majestic calmness, that gave no other invitation than its own voiceless security. In an instant he was clinging to it, climbing its craggy sides. Once secure upon its summit, he watched the waters gain upon and at last cover the sand where he had lately stood.

Through the entire night the wind blew violently, and he had to cling to his rock that he might not be blown off. Then, louder than the voice of the gale, the neglected words of a "Surer Rock" of salvation sounded in his ears, and God saw fit through the terrible lesson to teach His blessed Truth.

The next morning early, boats came out in search of mariners, and Gilbert was taken exhausted back to his home of mourning.

"God does not err," said the faithful wife. "He

has blessed me in making both husband and son find Him, though upon distant shores."

Gilbert supplied, as well as a good son could, his father's place, and thereafter passed his long life by the sea whose heaviest storm and blackest waters—even those of the River of Death—found him safe beside the higher Rock.

[5 April 1866]   FLAKE WHITE

Image from the *Christian Observer*, 24 March 1886

Our Light

We are all in some degree luminous, and have around us a little system, which it is no less our duty to brighten than it is the sun's duty to lighten his. Much of our want of usefulness arises from our discontent at the limited spheres in which God has ordained us to act. We had all much rather burn with a radiance that would set a whole horizon aglow, than, like a dark lantern, possess a gleam which God would use to lighten only the face of some benighted child. But let us to our humble work, nobly knowing that

> Thy love
> Shall chant itself in its own beatitudes,
> After its own lifeworking. A child's kiss
> Set on thy dying lips, shall make thee glad;
> A poor man served by thee, shall make thee rich;
> A sick man helped by thee, shall make thee
> strong.

Moro was a little water-carrier, the humblest of his class, whose labor consisted in a monotonous round with his panniered mule, and whose amusement was various modes of tantalizing the said animal. His mother, an infirm old woman, was his only remaining parent, and supporting her—if a bare subsistence might be called a support—was the only duty he thought he owed her. To obey her requests, to cheer her old age and loneliness, were duties of which he never thought. He was ignorant that, as the winter of age was chillingly shutting out the world from her, God had intended that through him she should enjoy another spring.

Moro came in late one evening and, wearied with the heat of the day, threw himself upon the floor near the low window. He was fast closing his sleepy eyes, when his mother said, "Did you bring me the herbs, Moro? I've been thinking about them all day."

"No, I forgot 'em," he replied peevishly.

"I don't believe you ever intend to do any thing I ask you," his mother said meekly. "You ain't doing much good in this world."

"I am as good a water-carrier as any," he replied.

"Yes, but that ain't all God put you here to do," his mother answered, and to the little humble boy came meditation instead of sleep, and for the first time he saw life in a sterner but more satisfactory light.

Moro's serious view did not influence him for the better immediately, for old habits are tenacious, and two days passed, in spite of his good resolutions, before he remembered his mother's herbs and took them to her. Feeling very genial in the knowledge of that good deed done, he paused late in the evening under the cool shade of a large tree that grew in the yard across the street. Looking there, he saw upon the ground at the foot of the tree, a boy about his age, but much smaller. The boy's sallow face and frail body often called forth the jeers of more fortunate lads—jeers in which Moro had sometimes joined. But this morning the crooked body leaning against the tree had a mute appeal that reached Moro's sympathies as it had never done before. Gently, he approached the boy.

"What do you do with yourself all the time, Little One?" asked Moro.

The boy looked up timidly for a moment and then answered, "Oh, nothing, just lie in the shade when it's hot, and the sun when it's cool, reading. I wish I was a water-carrier." He looked with yearning eyes from his own neatly clothed but small person, to the strongly knit but poorly clad figure of Moro.

"Well, I shouldn't like to be sick, but I wish I could read."

"Yes," said the boy. "Books tell many pleasant things, but I want to cross that field and climb those great rocks yonder. Have you ever been there?"

"Yes," replied Moro, and for quarter of an hour he stood telling Ferdinand about his journeys over the mountain.

"I wish you didn't have to go," said Ferdinand when Moro started off, "I like to hear you talk."

"Oh, I'll come again," Moro replied, "and if you like music, I will bring my guitar and sing for you," and with a stroke of his cudgel to quicken his slow mule, Moro was off, leaving not only the pleasant impression made by a few kind words, but an exciting anticipation, which meant a great deal to the poor sick child whose days were all so much alike.

Before sunset Ferdinand was out in the yard again, waiting for Moro. He waited until his eyes grew heavy. At last he fell asleep and dreamed that he entered suddenly into a cave so high the dome looked misty and its rocky sides stretched out illimitably. A gloomy twilight pervaded, except in some places where the stars on the foreheads of the people who filled the cave threw a brightness around. It would have all been bright with these stars, but many of the people wore veils over them. All those near Ferdinand were veiled, and his path was so dark that he often stumbled and fell. Once when he had fallen, he felt himself tenderly raised, and as he looked up, a little child with a star, like a miner's light on his brow, stood over him, and clasping his hand, walked with him. Just as the child, with its gentle face raised to him, asked why he wore his star veiled, a noise startled him.

Ferdinand awoke to a shouting boy who stood over his mule, whose thundering gallop had ended in a fall. Moro's mule had fallen upon and crushed one of his panniers, over which he was loudly lamenting.

"I say, come here," cried Ferdinand several times before Moro heard him.

"What shall I do?" he cried.

"I have some money to buy a new book, but you can have it," Ferdinand said.

Moro gratefully accepted it, on condition that he might repay when he could, and scampered off to make his purchase.

While Moro was buying his pannier, Ferdinand sat trying to separate his late dream from his late act, but the child with the star helping him, and his helping Moro, were inseparable. "I expect it is so," he thought, "I ought to have been helping somebody before, but have kept my light veiled."

Moro's pannier bought, his mule put up, and the successful termination of the accident having been told his mother, he took down his little old brown guitar and returned to Ferdinand. There, seated near him, he sang simple songs that charmed his hearer.

After that, every evening Moro came to sing for Ferdinand, teaching him at the same time, and Ferdinand teaching him to read in return. After a while Moro would often tempt Ferdinand to let him lift him upon his mule. Walking close to his friend, Moro would take him across the fields and to the foot of the craggy hills, until a glow of health came into Ferdinand's cheek, and the light of happiness into his eye. The bond of friendship strengthened between them; and Ferdinand's dream which he told to Moro, and of which they often spoke, taught them both what they afterwards learned more clearly from their Bibles, to "let their light shine before men."

HUNTSVILLE, ALA.   FLAKE WHITE
[14 June 1866]

FOUGHT AND WON

A long sultry summer day was closing in with mellow twilight that, softly deepening, was gradually peopling the purple sky with stars, and filling the lonely woods and roads with shadows. Now in the shadow, and now in the sheen of its uncertain light, two silent, weary travellers took their way down a desolate road. It brought them footsore and travel-stained to the bottom of a rocky hill, and there branched to the right and left, leaving in its fork a pleasant grassy spot upon which they both dropped themselves weariedly. First unstrapping the heavy peddler's packs that had galled their aching shoulders all day, they prepared to take their rest for the night.

The younger of the two threw himself upon his back and, with a sigh of relief, bared his brow to the evening wind that in a few moments fanned him to sleep. He was a pale, ragged boy of small growth, and clothes so much smaller that the numerous rents filling them might be looked upon rather as necessary provisions for locomotion than ragged misfortunes. A single glance at the little dirty, ugly figure proclaimed him one of those woeful children who knows no childhood—who believes only in the sinfulness of life because he has never seen its purity, and who, having caught no early vision of Heaven from his fond mother's lips, soon grows old and hardened in the unhallowed mould the world sets about him.

The other traveller was a low, ugly, scowling man, who immediately after settling himself upon the grass, took from his pocket a coarse supper, which he fell to eating with a carnivorous fierceness that reminded one very uncomfortably of "Riding Hood's" wolf. Resting his head on his pack, he was allowing the evening silence to lull him to sleep, when it was broken by the tread of a horse descending the hill. A moment after it stopped, the rider, an old man, asked which road led to Ramsey. He had not come that way before, he added, and did not know the direction. The peddler scowled from under his ragged old cap at the mild face above him, and then pointing with his finger, as blunt as his voice, to the left road, said, "That's it," and turned to sleep again.

Young Roger, wakened by the voices, sat up, and looked thoughtfully after the old man as he disappeared down the road. He then turned a look of disgust upon the creature by his side, who in the companionship of their wandering lives, he had known to commit every sin from a theft to maliciously misdirecting a benighted traveller. A new mood seemed to have come upon the young boy tonight and, looking back from the peddler to the road again, he presently sprang forth to his feet and, disappearing in the shadows, was soon speeding after the traveller. It was some time before his willing but weary steps brought Roger to the traveller. It was not until he lay a hesitating hand on the horse's bridle that the old man was aware of the boy's presence.

"You are on the wrong road for Ramsey, sir," Roger said, "I could not tell you back yonder," indicating the peddler behind him "but the other fork is the right one."

"Thank you, my boy," said the old man, as he turned his horse, and taking a small coin from his pocket, handed it to Roger.

"I didn't do it for money," returned the boy almost gruffly, for he was hurt at having his rare honesty misjudged and, drawing back, gave the road to the horse who, trotting quickly away, left him standing alone.

Alone, indeed! For by some strange impulse Roger now determined to cut himself off from his old dishonest life, and to begin another—though he had not a single friend in the world of honesty to lend him a helping hand. As he stood thus in the starry twilight, looking thoughtfully and much perplexed, his eyes presently made out on the ground before him, just where the horse had lately stood, a large leather purse.

In a moment, he had opened it and had seen the wealth it contained—and the riddle of the future that had so perplexed him luck seemed to have solved. He stood long and motionless gazing at it; the woods were very still, but seemed to grow more profoundly so, as the warfare between right and wrong began to wage in the boy's heart. He knew the owner of the purse was the old man, but he also knew that he needed the money more himself, and thus he reasoned, while the stars silently watched the contest and saw right triumphant at last. Slowly turning into the woods that he might not come upon his old companion again, Roger travelled until he was out of the trees and safely on the road to Ramsey; then he lay down to sleep.

The whole of the next day, he trudged patiently through hot dust and stones that blistered and tore his feet. A sultry sun beat sickeningly upon his head, and at nightfall, hungry and fainting, he sank down in the rank grass beside a wayside pool, and plunging his feet into its coolness soon fell asleep. When he awoke the next morning, there was mingled with the sound of insects around him, bells, and the low hum of city labor wafting from Ramsey, whose spires rose just beyond him above the trees.

Roger's wandering life had never happened to bring him to Ramsey before, and so much more friendless and lonely did it seem than the country he had just left, that for the first time he almost wished for the familiar old pack on his shoulders.

Late in the day, he was standing absently in front of a large store when among its faces, quickly going and coming, he saw the old traveller. In a moment, Roger's hand was on his arm and the purse delivered up, while the breathless old man looked astounded, as if honesty were a new gunpowder invention. He held the old purse very much as if he had never seen it before. He *had* seen it before though, as his kindly smile soon signified. Straightway, he led Roger into the store and showed him its dazzling wonders. There, as soon as his ragged clothes were exchanged for neat ones, Roger's new life began, and that first contest fought and gained out under the stars alone, made him strong for the future trials that crowd the Battle of Life.

[21 April 1869]   FLAKE WHITE

The Amen of the Stones

Photo by Linda Wright Riley

The Amen Of The Stones

"Well," said Uncle Allen at last, as he kindly stroked Eva's brown curls and looked into her beseeching face, "you are welcome to have this poor class that you have been teasing me about, but how long before you will be quite tired of it and wishing the children out of your sight?"

"Never, Uncle, never," Eva answered impulsively.

"People older than you, Eva, who call themselves Christians, tire of good works as soon as the novelty wears off," Uncle Allen returned with a touch of harsh scorn in his voice; and off he went, leaving the shade on Eva's face that his scoffing bitterness so often imprinted there. Her young Christian ardor was often sorely tried by his skepticism, as he, like all other doubters, used the rents in his own threadbare faith to spy his neighbor's errors through.

So Eva formed her long cherished class and taught them several times a week in the old unused library. When she had nothing more interesting to do and they all came with bright shining faces, she quite enjoyed it and thought she was playing Lady Bountiful in a very praiseworthy manner indeed. Meanwhile, Uncle Allen silently watched, to see her tire of her Samaritanism, and so "fulfill the words spoken by the prophet."

One soft balmy evening, that had followed a day of spring rain, Eva settled herself luxuriantly in the deep recess of the quiet old library window, rested her richly lettered book of "Legends" on its broad ledge, and prepared for an evening of undisturbed enjoyment. The room seemed all her own, for she had not perceived Uncle Allen on a dark sofa in the corner. There was nothing to mar her smiling repose, unless it be an early robin singing in the bare tree outside. Presently a touch on the arm startled her, and turning, she beheld one of her pupils with primer in hand. The demure little scholar in her bonnet, but barefooted, was not at all in keeping with the poetic spring robin or the splendid book.

"Why, dear me, Bessie, it has rained so hard all day, I did not think my class would come, and it's after the time now."

"I know it, Miss Eva, but I could not come sooner."

A slanting ray of low sunshine trembled through the leafless tree, as if the robin's warble shook it, and fell on Eva's gold and color-bordered book. She looked at it for a moment, then said, with a ring of sharp impatience in her voice, "Why, Bessie, I can't take the whole evening with just one scholar. Goodbye, I hope it will be bright so all can come next time," and so dismissed the sorrowful little scholar without looking up to mark how her face had clouded.

Bessie turned and slowly went out back the long, wet lane and into the cottage where she had finished all her work before going to Miss Eva, that she might not only say her lesson but get a book that her young teacher had promised to send sick Joe.

"You are back quick, Bessie," said Joe as he raised his pale face from the pillow. He held out his hand for the book.

"Yes, Joe, but Miss Eva could not attend to me this evening. There was only me, one, you see."

"There were the two of us if she had only remembered me," said Joe, dropping back, "I am so sorry," and then patiently said no more.

Eva turned over the leaves unheedingly for some moments after Bessie's dismissal, then presently stopped at a page wonderfully and most quaintly ornamented with a border of old stones, overgrown with moss and lichens in a manner that seemed to give each rock a grotesque face. Its strangeness made her smile till she commenced to read in its midst the following old Legend:

THE AMEN OF THE STONES

"Boys who enjoy 'fun' all the more when it is spiced 'with death to the frogs,' are common to all ages, their dust no doubt lying aside with Mastodon bones. One of these lads, ancient folks tell us, played his wild pranks in the time of Venerable Bede[1] with, no doubt, Elisha's forty-two[2] beside; nevertheless about only one does tradition speak with certainty.

"With this young Speedfoot, life was a jest; there was nothing so serious that it did not sing hollow to his laugh and, be it kindly fun or cruel, he frolicked time away. By some strange chance this Ignis Fatuus[3] became the erratic guide to this old preacher, Venerable Bede who, like another John the Baptist, was crying in the wilderness. Through hamlet, town and city, and forests that lay between, the strange couple took their way. Speedfoot carelessly guided the feet of the old blind man, whose eyes God seemed to have closed upon the world that he might turn them upon an inward vision of heaven.

"One day the old Preacher had stopped long at an hamlet where the poor folk drank in his wisdom with great eagerness. The long detention and the much weeping and praying of the people had so sharply tried the mettlesome soul of young Speedfoot that his mischief broke bounds the first wood they entered. Here, in passing a little valley covered with stones, Speedfoot, choking with mirth, said, 'Father, stop, more congregations await to hear you in this place.' Sitting down

[1] Venerable Bede (c.673-735). An English scholar and historian.
[2] The 42 children who taunted the prophet Elisha (2 Kings 2:23-25).
[3] Ignis Fatuus. Flickering lights over a swamp. Anything deceptive.

upon one of the scattered stones, he waited with trembling eyes to hear a sermon delivered to the rocks. Instantly the godly old man halted and broke the silence of the woods with such a stream of eloquence as angels might have bent ears earthward to hear, then raising his trembling arms and tearful blind eyes to heaven, he prayed that chiefest piece of supplicating eloquence, 'Our Father,' and when the last petition had sounded, lo! the quiet woods rang with a thousand voices as the listening stones cried back 'Amen.' Down upon his knees in the deep fern fell Speedfoot, with his old heart of stone become one of flesh: broken and contrite, desiring henceforth to do our Father's will."

There was a wistful, sorrowful look in Eva's penitent eyes, as she raised them from the quaint old legend. "We should never withhold God's seed," she murmured, "for He can even make words spoken to stones touch a heart somewhere. Oh God! Bessie! Forgive me!"

A low "Amen" beside her was added to her sobbing prayer, and Eva was taken into her Uncle's arms. "I saw your fault, Eva, and I witnessed your repentance, and the sight of a Christian's penitence has done me good." He kissed her gently and sat down before the window to read her blessed Legend, while she ran in the fading sunset down to Bessie, to say a word of encouragement and kindness and to leave the neglected book with sick Joe.

[23 June 1869]   FLAKE WHITE

Image from the *Christian Observer*, 9 October 1878

A Ministry Of Love
Let Your Light So Shine

Ellen Maxwell's morning work was done. Having long since given her father his breakfast and seen him off to work, she set the plain little home into dainty order. There remained nothing more to be done but to put her brother Felix in his armchair near a favorite window, with his crutches in reach. At last, she was ready for her shopping.

She put on her shawl and hat, kissed Felix goodbye, and took her way down the busy street. As she went along, she could not help but to think of poor lame Felix. His life, full of longings for beautiful happy things, was yet an emptier one than her own for he was cut off from the beauties of nature that were open to her. Her eyes, ever ready for a stray bit of loveliness, lifted themselves to the trees where the green mist of tender spring leaves was forming against the soft gray sky that gleamed in April brightness.

A warm drop of rain presently fell upon her upturned face and brought her back to practical things. She quickened her lagging steps—but in vain. She was still far from her destination as the drops increased till a shower of shining rain sent her into a convenient porch for shelter.

She had stood there but a moment, when the door opened and a pleasant voice said, "The rain sweeps through the porch. Come inside till the shower is over."

Ellen followed the kind voice and found herself in a room pervaded by a delicious air of refinement in its tinted walls, mellow pictures, misty curtains, busts, vases, books, and the thousand graceful adornments so dear to one sensitive to beautiful surroundings.

"Have a seat," said Mrs. May who had taken her own seat near a window ledge graced by a basket of flowers. "You see, I was just going out myself when the rain prevented me, too. I was going to take these flowers to a home where a little child died yesterday."

Ellen stooped for a moment over the nest of lilies of the valley fringed with fragrant leaves, then said impulsively, "Ah, how many living people there are to whom such flowers would be very, very precious!" She paused abruptly as she met a startled look from her hostess. "Pardon me, I do not mean that it is not beautiful to give flowers to the dead, but there are many living who need their ministry more."

"Do you love flowers so well, then?" asked the lady.

"Everyone does, I suppose," replied Ellen almost evasively. "I have a brother who carves flowers in wood quite lovingly." She rose and said, "the rain is over now, I think."

"Yes," replied the lady taking up her flowers and leading the way out. As they passed down the street together, she studied her companion somewhat curiously until Ellen paused with a polite "Good morning, and thank you," and disappeared in the shop for which she was bound.

Mrs. May passed on to the house of mourning where she delivered her flowers, then returned slowly, her mind still busy thinking of Ellen. "Her dress is as mean as many of my poor, though she would not accept a garment or a loaf of bread. And yet—" asserted Mrs. May to herself, "—I am sure she is poor in many things, and needs some sort of charity more then many on my list. Ah! There she is again!" and a moment more she was beside Ellen who, having done her errand, was coming out of the shop.

"I am glad we meet again," said Mrs. May, "I want you to take me to see your brother's carvings, if you are going back home, and think he will not object."

"I am sure not," said Ellen gently, adding a few words descriptive of Felix's patient life, which brought them to his door.

"I have brought this lady to see your last carving, Felix," Ellen said, when they were in the cripple's room, which was scrupulously clean but bare as a cell, except for the wall near his chair where many little objects hung, all cut by the lame boy's thin hands.

"And this," thought Mrs. May, glancing round the plain room, "is where with enough to eat, these two young souls are starving!" In self-rebuke, her thoughts flew to her own beautiful house and her neighbors', which, in selfish seclusion "carried their light like a jewel, not giving it out like a star!"

"Your carvings are very pretty and promising," she said to Felix, after a cordial examination of them, "but you must not copy picture-flowers any more. I have a whole hothouse of flowers waiting to be copied, and will send you a bunch tomorrow if your sister will come and select them for you."

Ellen and Felix always remembered that next day as a new era. And to Mrs. May it was like a revelation, watching Ellen's long subjected raptures pour over her flowers. Her sheaf of lilies, so like the bunch gathered yesterday, now seemed to cheer a brother and his sister in yet a "more excellent way."

"Here is a charming magazine, too," she said as Ellen was leaving, "I have finished reading it."

"Thank you," said Ellen, thinking how often she had looked longingly at these in the bookseller's window, and then continued after a moment's hesitation, "When we are done reading it, may I lend it to poor Miss Paul? She teaches school next us, and loves books, and has so few."

"Certainly," said Mrs. May, "I do not want it again."

"Then it will travel a long way!" cried Ellen, running down the steps.

"Yes, travel a long way!"

Several weeks passed and Mrs. May was leaving her home one morning when she met at the steps a lady friend of somewhat lofty aspect, as indeed befitted her office as president of the "Ladies' Aid Society." She soon inquired what Mrs. May, as a member of that same body had been doing since they met last.

"Oh, I have been busy in a new direction," Mrs. May answered.

"Ah!" cried the president, eagerly bringing out her pencil and book, "Where, in the small-pox district?"

"No," said Mrs. May, "in a clean healthy neighborhood, where there are few if any beggars. I am going there now to leave this fashion book," she ended with a ripple of laughter. "I have a young friend who though a very poor girl can make her own new dress. She has as true an eye for form and color as you or I, and this book of patterns, which she is not able to buy, will help her greatly."

"I have learned lately," Mrs. May continued with sweet gravity, "that there are a great many people in the world hungry for something beside loaves and fishes. When we pray for those who are 'distressed in mind, body or estate,' we patrons of charity take care of the 'body and estate,' but tend to neglect the 'mind.' I don't know what we mean by feeding the hungry body back to life, if we do not also feed the mind."

Mrs. May never forgot her duty to absolute suffering and poverty; but many a book, paper, flower, box of colors, or piece of music found its way through her ministry of "whatsoever things are lovely" into the hands of people not greatly lacking in food or raiment, but needy nevertheless. Thus she strove henceforth to reach and comfort her peculiar "poor," believing that God meant for the light of her culture to shine in His service as well as her gold.

HUNTSVILLE, ALA.   FLAKE WHITE
[22 March 1876]

GERALDINE'S WINDOW
A Story of a Quiet Life
By Flake White

Aspen was one of the loveliest streets in the city where Geraldine Marr lived; in one of its prettiest blocks was her home, a quaint, old-fashioned red brick house standing not immediately on the street, but back a step with an iron railing in front. This was an arrangement that afforded Geraldine—being a confirmed invalid—no little satisfaction. Her chief outlook into the world was her chamber window, and it would not have suited her half so well had it either been put on the street, or yet any further back.

She had been homebound for years and in the day never left the large chair that stood in the cozy recess of the low, broad front window, always known as "Geraldine's Window." Here, the quivering shadows from the friendly aspens fell kindly in the summer, and the pale sunshine came cheerfully in the window, while people passing ceaselessly were watched day after day by thoughtful Geraldine. So this window became the center of her world.

When in the bloom of her girlhood, she had waked from a long illness to a knowledge of the fact that health was gone forever, and that henceforth she was to exchange the bright world outside for the pain and monotony of a sick-chamber, she had rebelled long and bitterly. She never in all her afterlife forgot the day upon which that rebellion finally ended, and her cross seemed suddenly light enough for her to carry.

That day she was lying upon her bed, gloomy and spiritless, when the door of her darkened chamber opened noiselessly. Hannah, their old servant who had answered a ring at the front door, put her head in and said timidly, "Please, Miss Geraldine, your mother is out. Will you see this person? She has some fancy knitting to sell."

The woman and little child who were ushered into the dim room came softly to the sick girl's bed and placed beside her a basket of fleecy knitted articles.

"You need not have troubled me," said Geraldine feebly, with a gesture of habitual impatience. "I am never to be well again, never again! And you can show me nothing that I want."

There was an instant pause, while the woman quietly took in this response. When at last she spoke, it was in a voice so full of steady sweetness that it claimed Geraldine's ear at once.

"Believe me, a life like yours seems something wonderful. It is a life set apart, consecrated to holy uses. Lighthouses are stationary, but they do as much service as lifeboats. Take comfort, my child, it will not always be so hard for you; it is to darkened lives that God has promised there shall be 'songs in the night.' "

Geraldine listened till the voice, the sweetest she had ever heard, ceased; and then, after a moment, she took from their basket two little filmy shawls of different colors and held them off at some length, asking, "Which of them do you call prettier? I will take your choice."

There was not an answer for a moment, but then with a smile, the woman replied, "I do not see them; I am blind."

Geraldine's arm dropped, and she turned to the serene, nay, the happy face beside her, and said, "I thought you did not talk to me as others do—but as one who knows. Yours, too, is a life set apart."

There were a few more quiet words between them, and then, paying for the two shawls, Geraldine bade her visitors goodbye and saw them depart.

The rest of the day was a very thoughtful one for Geraldine. She told her mother, when she came in, only that a wonderful, happy blind woman had visited her.

The next morning she asked to be placed in her chair and to have the window opened.

"Perhaps I shall see the happy blind woman pass," she said.

And so the next day and the next, she sat at the low, broad window and scanned the busy passers-by; but the woman was not among them, nor indeed did Geraldine ever see her again.

As time went on, the blind woman became less a reality to Geraldine than a sort of divine vision who had entered her darkened room and life, and had shown her the light that would become the motive for her life. She never forgot the value of those few words spoken in season to her own soul, and henceforth tried to make her shrouded life, thus "set apart," shine for other

> Forlorn and shipwrecked brethren,
> Who, seeing, might take heart again.

[14 June 1876]

GERALDINE'S WINDOW
A Friend in Need
BY FLAKE WHITE

At the head of Aspen Street, there was a boys' school, to and from which the scholars used to troop past Geraldine's window, making her mornings cheerful by the vision of their shining faces. In the evenings she could sympathize at the sight of the same faces all wearied with a day of tasks and childish vexations; but she never failed to give to these little tired ones a smile as they passed—which, God knows, may have taken the place of a mother's smile to more than one child, for whom there was the light of no mother's smile at home.

There was one boy she watched with peculiar interest. He was always ragged, though clean, always in a hurry and always studying. He went to school before any of the other boys, and came back after them. In cold weather, he always carried a bundle of lightwood in the hand that did not hold a book.

Sometimes, to Geraldine's amusement, the boy walked along preparing his speeches and, forgetful of everything around him, would mutter and gesticulate in rapt abandon. Upon reaching his peroration, he would pause and make his bow as gravely as if upon the rostrum. Only the sudden dropping of his book or lightwood, or the sharp elbow of a passer-by would remind him where he was, and send him along in a scamper.

It was no wonder that thoughtful Geraldine had, from her quiet post, long watched this curious boy and speculated upon his history. In truth, this David was a poor orphan boy, alone in the city, trying to support and educate himself. Wholly unable to pay his way at school, he had considered himself a lad of exceptional good fortune when he found the principal of the Aspen Street School willing to allow him a pupil's place in exchange for his services in making fires and bringing water for the school.

Conscious of a large amount of unemployed energy, he felt no work was too hard, if he could only go to school; so he had started with high hopes. But, alas, he had not wisely counted the cost. His duties took up much of the time he should have given to study. Except one book that he owned, he had to study from books borrowed day after day from his comrades. As the winter grew on, his duties increased and his time for study lessened. His impatient master scolded—calling the naturally bright lad at one time a genius and, at another, a dunce until the boy felt his spirits breaking and his energies giving way.

On a certain cold, rainy afternoon, David waited after school, as he always did, hoping to be able to borrow from some less studious boy the books he needed for the night. Quite a group lingered about the fire, drawing on their overcoats and caps preparatory to starting home. Tired with waiting, David laid his hand on the shoulder of a lad who sat with his feet lazily hoisted on the stove, and said, "Come, hurry up, Miles. I know you are done with your algebra book for this evening."

"Yes," said Miles, good-naturedly closing his book. "I will lend it to you, slate and all, if you will do a take-off of Little Hugo for us."

Poor, tired David hesitated, looked at the book, then swallowed his reluctance. And in only a moment he ceased to be David and became Little Hugo, the Aspen School drawing master, whose odd manners and broken English made him the butt of the students. David fastened the lowest button of his tight jacket, drew down his ragged cuffs, and tucked up his collar with an air so comically like the veritable Hugo, that the delighted boys greeted it with a din of applause, to which David cried, "Stop! Who made dot kick?" in the absurd words used by Mr. Hugo to the boys when they treated him to such a storm.

Then behold, the half-open door was flung wide and in stepped Mr. Hugo followed by a stranger. In a flash every boy had disappeared save poor David, himself again, but wishing he was anybody else. Now the picture of penitence, he cried, "Forgive me, Mr. Hugo. I only did it to get a book."

"Pooh! Pooh!" cried a stranger, bustling in ahead of Mr. Hugo, "I am very much obliged to you for it. I am manager of the Globe Theatre, where Mr. Hugo is painting us some scenes, and being in want of a boy to fill a vacancy, he spoke to me of you, and brought me to see you. What do you say to leaving school, and coming on the boards? I will make it worth your while. Come with Mr. Hugo the day after tomorrow."

And not waiting for a reply, the busy manager and Mr. Hugo turned away and left him. David stood like one in a dream, till the increasing cold and dark of the deserted schoolroom reminded him to lock up and go home. Of course, in his sudden exit, Miles had made off with the coveted book, and so the evening was spent in thinking rather than studying.

The next day was the most exasperating one poor David had ever spent. His thin ragged clothes let in the bitter cold, his master scolded at his unlearned lessons—and when the day was done, David's struggle for an education was over. He determined to accept the manager's offer. This difficult decision was made along Aspen Street.

To emphasize it David paused, raised his determined face and quickly threw, as far as he could send it—into the gutter with a splash—the one book that had been his own.

The little tragedy chanced to take place just in front of Geraldine's window. She saw it at a glance, and tapped on the window. Her white finger beckoned David. A moment later, he stood in her presence. "I have just written a note," she said, "which I want delivered this evening. Can you take it for me?"

"Yes, ma'am," replied David softly, to suit the gentle lady and the quiet, fragrant room.

"It is to my uncle, Mr. White, the book-seller, whom I ask for a book." But here Geraldine turned a grave look upon David. "You must not throw it away as you did a book just now. Why was that?"

Poor, perplexed David stammered a moment and then with a sob in his throat, brokenly told Geraldine his story.

"I am glad you gave up just here," she responded in an earnest tone, "since it gives me a chance to point out to you a better life than a comedian's."

She then opened her note, added a few lines to ask her uncle if he could not find employment for David in his great publishing house. Mr. White, who was always a ready helper in gentle Geraldine's schemes of usefulness, willingly did as she requested—and never had cause to regret it.

David's fine nature expanded beautifully in a life of congenial, steady work. He grew daily in the confidence and esteem of his employer and the affection of Geraldine, who never had a warmer friend than David proved to be, for he brought in her quiet life the audacity of his youth, with its hopes, ambitions and sunny energy. While she, ever ready with counsel and sympathy, continued to shine upon him, steadfast like a star.

[21 June 1876]

GERALDINE'S WINDOW
Phillis' Story
BY FLAKE WHITE

Close beside a little ivy-grown church that stood in one of the quaintest old portions of the town where Geraldine lived, there was an humble sexton's house. Steeped forever in the church's shadow, the small cottage seemed to take from it a consecrated look—peaceful and unworldly—for in its low window were displayed groups of rude plaster casts of rapturous angels and kneeling saints, by the sale of which the old sexton helped eke out a scanty living.

Holding a tray of these plaster figures, old Joseph stood one morning at his door, preparing to go out. He looked back for a moment to say goodbye to his little daughter, Phillis, who was flitting about the neat kitchen at her morning's work, her blue dress and white neckerchief setting her face and dark eyes into a bonny picture.

"Take heart, Phillis," the old sexton said. "I save a little every few days, and if I should have good luck today, we may soon go back to our old home, where thy good sister will make thee and thy old father happy."

So off he went, planning the happy time—as he had for years—while he tried to save enough from their daily living to take Phillis back to where all his children had been born and where his oldest daughter and her husband lived "at the old mill." In this way, when he died, Phillis might not be left among strangers.

Round and round old Joseph walked all day but selling nothing. Stumbling home weary and discouraged, he talked late to Phillis about going home. Even as he fell asleep, he muttered of the old place, where he seemed in dreams to be meeting his wife and children gone before, as perhaps he was—for, in the morning, Phillis' father was dead.

For days, poor Phillis was stricken quite mute and helpless. But when the new sexton's family moved into the house, she had to look about for work to do and another home, even though they gave her leave to stay there until she found another. Her heart longed to leave the lonely city and go to her sister, but the money so carefully accumulated for that purpose by her father had been kept in a nook unknown to her, and there was no finding it now. Nothing was to do but work her own way there.

So, one morning the desolate girl shook off the languor of her grief and taking up her father's old tray, filled it with a group of his plaster figures and started out to sell them. All day she walked about without a sale until toward evening her tired feet brought her slowly down Aspen Street.

Geraldine's low, broad window was open and looked like a bower with its draperies of misty white curtains and flower-bright ledge. In the midst of it enshrined, sat the quiet figure of Geraldine herself. Homeless Phillis cast a despondent look there, which changed to a glad one when Geraldine asked her to bring in her figures.

"Have I not seen you pass before—sometimes with an old man, who used to carry these?" asked Geraldine, who never forgot a face that had interested her.

Phillis, kneeling low that Geraldine might see better her figures, told her little story. Geraldine, deeply interested, gave her kind words and a good price for one of her clumsy little vases, then sent her home comforted.

It was indeed a very clumsy vase, though she had not bought it for its beauty, Geraldine explained, as her mother removed it from the window to set out of sight as soon as Phillis was gone. But no sooner had she picked up the unexpectedly heavy vase than it fell with a crash, and out rolled old Jacob's hoardings—a handful of coins, crooked pence and worn coppers, all of which would seem a little fortune to Phillis.

That night when Phillis got home, the new sexton saw that she had sold only one image all day. "That will never do," he said.

So she determined to pluck up courage for the next day and find another way to Janet's. "At least I'll not beg. I'll *sing* my way," she said.

The next morning, she dressed herself as neatly as possible and started on her weary pilgrimage. She made her way straight through the city, singing low and timidly at windows where she saw the friendly faces of little children, and now and then was given a penny for her pathetic ballads. She was glad as she neared the lady Geraldine's window, and when she reached it, she paused and began to sing a little air her father had loved.

"Oh, Mother! Mother! It is the image girl!" cried Geraldine, all aglow with the excitement that this little drama lent her quiet life. "Do bring her in."

And when the little singer stood before her, Geraldine showed her the broken vase and poured into her lap the coins it had contained.

It is hard to say who was happier—rapturous Phillis or quiet Geraldine, who from her "life set apart" had learned to find happiness through the eyes of others.

Without further trouble, Phillis made her way to her sister's home and from there wrote a quaint little letter to Geraldine, who kept it always as one of her treasures.

"You will be glad to know," the letter said, "that I am safe with my sister and happy; and before you forget little Phillis, I would like to tell you what a help you were to me—helpful when you bought our wares, and when you simply smiled on us from your window. I often walked past it in the evening just to see your gentle face before I slept. It seems to shine on me still."

Folding up the letter, Geraldine sat thinking of her years, so enriched with peace and quiet usefulness. She thanked God for the blind woman who had first bade her take courage, knowing that there is no life so denied but He will grant it a harvest—even if its seeds are but smiles to the tearful and words of comfort to the troubled.

[28 June 1876]

Courtesy of Burritt Museum and Park

"Thou and I together, Nell"

Editorial Note

Howard Weeden published four silhouettes in Charles
Dickens' novel, *The Old Curiosity Shop.*[1]   The above one
represents the characters of the old man and Nell.

---

[1]   New York: D. Appleton and Co., 1873.

GERALDINE'S WINDOW
Paul's Silhouette

BY FLAKE WHITE

The neighbors along Aspen Street often had occasion to regret the frequency with which old Dr. Ashton's buggy was seen standing at Geraldine's door. His presence there indicated that a heavier cross of suffering than usual was being laid upon their patient friend. But his visits were in fact mingled with pleasure both for the doctor and his patient, as he, having been her physician since childhood, loved her as tenderly as his reserved nature could love anyone. While she, with her heaven-given power of seeing the best in everyone, clearly saw and loved him.

The doctor came in one cold morning as Geraldine was just recovering from one of her attacks and found her much better and sitting up at her window.

"It is a pleasure to be up again," she said to him. "And oh, I've had my sympathies so aroused this morning, watching that little ragged boy there across the street who is trying to thaw his frozen fingers over a barrel of warm ashes. See how wretchedly cold he looks."

"My charity practice introduces me to quite enough of those street children," responded the doctor. "And I think you had better stop looking out of this window if it always has the effect of 'arousing your sympathies.' "

"Oh, it isn't as bad a feeling as you imagine," replied Geraldine with a pointed smile that the doctor found unanswerable. He presently took his leave and Geraldine found herself musing over this friend who was so kind to her but so cold to the world in general.

When she looked up again, she saw that the little ragged boy had come across the street and was standing in front of her window. As soon as he caught her eye, he eagerly thrust through the railings a pair of blue, half-frozen hands, in which he held a large pair of scissors. Taking out a sheet of black paper, he fell to cutting a figure with the most marvelous rapidity. As soon as it was done, Geraldine bade him bring it in, and found it to be a very splendid silhouette likeness of the doctor as he came out of the house—tall and somewhat pompous. "The sly artist has made my doctor, in his ample fur-lined cloak and ready cane, just the figure to strike terror in a homeless boy," Geraldine thought.

His name was Paul, he said; Paul Scissors, his comrades called him, because he had no means of living, save what cutting these figures bought him. He was thin and ragged and dirty, except his face; and his feet were bare upon the frozen ground.

Geraldine, after buying his figure, made him warm himself beside her bright fire, gave him the delicate lunch that stood untasted beside her chair, and saw him leave her, at last, with a face a trifle less pale and most grateful.

The next day when Dr. Ashton called, Geraldine showed him Paul's silhouette of himself. The doctor thought it excellent—but would take no interest in the boy, "The rascal will be here every day now and expect you to buy all the pictures he cuts."

And sure enough Paul came back every morning until, alas! he found the lady's window closed and heard, as he hung about the door, that she was sick again.

After hearing that, he came next day early, and stood close beside the steps till the doctor came, and as he was passing in, Paul laid a timid hand on his rich cloak and drew from his own bosom an early snowdrop. He prayed the doctor give it to the sick lady—"from Paul."

"He's an exceptional street child, I must confess," said the doctor with a smile, "he hardly swore at all when he sent you this flower!"

"Not at all, you mean," insisted Geraldine, whose simple heart went as directly as a sunbeam to the truth of things. "The child who sent me this—his all—would not swear."

By the time Geraldine was up once more the winter had slipped away, and spring had come, and though she was in her old seat at the window again, she saw Paul no more. She was wondering one morning what had become of him, when Hannah, answering a timid ring at the bell, ushered in a boy. In his raggedness, thinness and poverty, he was the *facsimile* of Paul, even with the snowdrop which he drew from his sleeve and gave to Geraldine.

"Paul Scissors, my pal, sent it to you," the boy said. "He has been sick this long time, and won't never get well no more. He ain't forgot you, though, and sent this flower, what growed in his window."

Geraldine took Paul's address, and the next day seeing Dr. Ashton, begged him to go and see the boy. Of course the doctor only grumbled a reply, but before night found himself at Paul's tenement, and climbing up a flight of crazy stairs, made his way into a long low room, still as death and unfurnished except for a number of small rough beds, all empty save one near a window— on which lay little Paul—now only a mere skeleton, weak-voiced and hollow-eyed.

"No; no home except this," he said in answer to the doctor's question; "and no mother; but I used to have one, when I was young," the boy said, with an odd sort of smile. "I had forgot how she looked, till I saw Miss Geraldine, and then I knew my mother looked like her smile!"

One bright summer morning some weeks after this, Geraldine sat listening to her old friend, David, who had just returned from a journey away up in the country, where he had been on business for Mr. White. He had come in to tell Geraldine that in his travels he had passed the home of Phillis, who had sent her back a letter, together with a hundred messages of love and grateful remembrance. While David described Phillis' simple and useful life—so much of whose peace, Geraldine had secured—the door opened and there was Dr. Ashton. To Geraldine's surprise, he was followed by Paul, the Scissors boy who was now recovered from his illness, his rags, and his poverty.

"This boy has such an eye for anatomy," said the doctor, "that I cured him and took him home to make another doctor of him."

Paul, lifting a grateful face to the doctor then turned and kneeling beside Geraldine, took her fair hand in his, and thanked her with tears more eloquent than words; while David impulsively knelt there, too.

Geraldine, turning a shining face upon the doctor, said: "Truly, my friend, the blind woman, spoke well—for it is to darkened lives that God gives 'songs in the night.' "

[12 July 1876]

Image from the *Christian Observer*, 16 January 1889

THE SHUT-IN TRAVELLERS

BY FLAKE WHITE

When the children first went to Dakota they thought Prairie Hall Farm the holiest place in the world, with its pretty house and barns and sunny fields set in the midst of broad prairies that rolled their green waves off to the edge of the world, and above them the blue heavens bending like the smile of God! But all too soon the summer vanished; the green and blue lights went out, and one day the world lay dead in a burial of snow.

It is hard to describe the desolation of those first snowbound days when for Howard and Sidney there were no more breezy rides on their ponies and for Louise no more sunlit frolics in the garden. But instead, with each monotonous day just like the last, the snow was so deep that they could neither go to friends, nor have friends come to them.

For a while, even Mamma looked grave and anxious, but one morning, after a night in which she had slept little and thought much, she came into the room where the children were idly gathered at their study table. She smiled so brightly that the little ones drew close to her, and asked her why.

"Well," said she, "it strikes me that we have grumbled long enough now about the snow and the loneliness and dear Papa's absence; so I propose that we all go to work to make things brighter. Suppose instead of sitting here, we travel?"

"What, bring out the ponies and ride away?" cried Sidney with shining eyes.

"Wait!" she answered. "If you want to get to the heart of things, riding there is not always the best way. Suppose we go this time on the shoulders of the men in the bookcases there? Let this bright room with its warm fires, its large round table and easy chairs be the world, and we, four happy travellers. Come, shall we go?" and the children sprang to their feet and cried that they were ready.

"Well, now," said Mamma, "the first step is to put a caution up on the wall. It is a rule from the hospital when all the children have the measles: THE ONLY WORDS SPOKEN IN THIS ROOM MUST BE KIND WORDS.

And when she had written the rule in large letters on a great strip of paper and tacked it up, they resumed their seats and planned their winter journeyings.

From that moment their days brightened; study became a fine art at Prairie Hall, and the most prosaic of the lessons were amiably learned in view of the pleasures that followed.

The last lesson was always geography, so that the great round table could be cleared of everything except geography for reference, and the great maps of the countries that Mamma had cut out of heavy paper. There was a busy time arranging these correctly, so that just the proper breadth of mahogany seas and oceans would lie between. Then Howard would bring out the wonder-box, filled with all sorts of seed, and neatly labeled. There were also little bags of coffee, tea, sugar, rice, wheat, indigo, spices, as well as samples of cotton, wool, linen, silk, hemp, paper, feathers and leather. These were carefully placed on their native countries. (Oh, you needed to be very knowing to get them just right.) Then would begin a game of commerce.

A paper boat would load with cotton at America and carry it to England, where it exchanged for hardware; cotton goods would ship to Australia and bring away wool; spices at Ceylon would exchange for Russian hemp and wheat. Other trade goods included oranges at Spain, carpets in Belgium, cheese in Denmark, watches in Switzerland, furs in Siberia, sandalwood in India, ostrich feathers and dates in Africa, olives and velvets in France, coffee in Brazil, silks and tea in China.

Sometimes there was excited confusion—when Sidney would go to England for cotton, or to Russia for oranges; and Howard would make a vain journey to Denmark for olives. But Mamma was at hand to turn to the geography book, and things were soon set right. Sometimes, too, the boat lost its way; or, if the roads were overland, Louise's doll-wagon would be overturned, but they bore their perils bravely, for there were many pleasures to counterbalance them. Oh, what pleasant talks they had about strange lands through which they wandered, till the orange-scented and spice-laden airs from the sunny orient blew upon them, and seemed to warm their snowbound home. After all, the real zones are in our hearts, and if they are warm, we may find the tropics anywhere.

The long evenings at Prairie Hall were charmingly shortened by meetings of the "Hans Christian Anderson Club." Mamma was its president, and the first evening she read a short life of this dear old lover of children, and showed the little ones how to cut his silhouette (big nose and tender smile) from black paper, and then to draw a map of Denmark with the little island of Funen where he was born. These were the first contributions to the Anderson Museum, which occupied a corner of the room, and which filled up rapidly after that. Each evening when a story was read something illustrative of it was added to the museum.

For instance, when Mamma read the "Little Match Girl," a match marked it; the "Darning Needle," a needle; "The Storks," a picture of storks; the "Ugly Duckling," a picture of a swan; "Five Out of One Shell," five peas. When they reached that funniest story of all, "What the Old Man Does is Always Right" quite a menagerie was required to illustrate it: a horse, a cow, a goose, a fowl, and a sack of apples! How merry an evening this made! Little Louise was generally asleep when the club met, but the next day when she was sure to go to the museum to see what had been added, Howard and Sidney were always ready to tell her the story.

Their club still continues its cozy meetings and will be glad to have all the little readers of the *Observer* join them, and each have a museum like the one at Prairie Hall.

Perhaps another time you may hear how the shut-in children spent their Sabbaths, and how they went with reverent feet to the Holy Land.

HUNTSVILLE, ALA.
[12 January 1887]

Image from the *Christian Observer*, 21 November 1877

A TELLTALE SCRAPBOOK

By Flake White

It was May Day and Polly's birthday. She was soon dressed and down in the dining room, where a great nosegay of violets glowed at her plate, bearing the good wishes of her little brother, Geoffrey. Beside it sat a large brown parcel bearing the love of her father and mother. The parcel contained a scrapbook, so long the desire of her heart. As soon as breakfast was over, she declared herself ready to begin making it at once.

"Wait," said her mother, "it will take you a good while to get ready for work. First, you must find a place to keep your book and pictures, and I think I have just the place you would like."

So off they went to the mother's room, where just under the honeysuckle window (as the children called it) stood a little old-fashioned table with a nice drawer.

"Here, Polly," said her mother, "you can keep your book and pictures. And here is a nice pair of scissors and a piece of soft, clean cloth to wipe the pages neatly when you have been using the paste—so that the leaves will not stick." She continued, "When you want to work you can make your own paste. Just put a tablespoon full of starch from the pantry into this tin cup and add a half-cup of cold water, then stir until it is dissolved. Then you can set it on the stove and stir until it boils. This is better than any kind of glue, as it does not darken with time."

Two or three weeks went by, and Polly's drawer was gathering quite a harvest of pictures, bits of poetry and good words. So one rainy Saturday she made a cup of paste and came into the room where her mother sat sewing on her knee in the old-fashioned way—not on a machine which raises such a din of noise between little children and their mothers. The two talked softly as Polly began her book.

The beginning was a hard matter, for Polly deemed the frontispiece a thing of great importance, and after a while settled upon a quaint, bright picture of Red Riding Hood whose sweet welcoming face smiling from under her crimson hood would seem to say, "Come in" as one opened the book. On the next page she put a lovely picture of a seashell, and under it this sweet bit of poetry, cut from an old paper:

Take the bright shell
From its home on the lea,
And wherever it goes,
It will sing of the sea.
So take the fond heart
From its home and its hearth,
'Twill sing of the loved
To the ends of the earth.

On the next page she put a picture of a "Wounded Drummer Boy" which she thought quite beautiful enough to adorn a eulogium in poetry but she could find no words suitable, so with a sudden bright thought, she said, "Mother, I believe I'll run over and get the Corporal to write a couplet under my picture."

Seizing her bonnet and book, she flew across the street to a little brown house where lived an old soldier, familiarly known as the Corporal. He had lost a leg in the war, and got many a sabre cut beside. Now he spent his peaceful days in making baskets for a living, and penning rhymes and stories for a pastime. These, and a thousand other charming things, made him the hero of the village children.

The Corporal laid down his willows the moment Polly put her curly head in his low window, then gladly wrote her couplet with a readiness and neatness that Polly considered magical. He admired her book very much, saying as he handed it back to her, "I used to have a scrapbook myself when I was a lad but," shaking his head dubiously, "it got too personal after awhile, and I had to give it up."

"How was that?" asked Polly, uneasily.

"Well, you see," answered the Corporal, "sometimes I would work on my book when I was in a bad humor, and the things would go down carelessly and then it would tell on me whenever I looked at it afterwards. But that won't be the way with you—little girls never do wrong!"

Polly ran home laughing. "I don't know about being good," she said to her mother, "but I know I won't put anything but goodness down in my pretty book."

However, as time went on Polly found that, like the Corporal, the badness would get into her book. For half a dozen pages all went well, but then came a page that Polly always hated to look at. She remembered the rainy day she had worked on that page when little Geoffrey had run over and cunningly put his curly head in her way. When she pushed him aside, his elbow had upset her paste-cup sending a horrid stream across her page.

In an instant, frightened Geoffrey was gone, and Polly after him. The chase once begun was not soon ended, for Geoffrey was quick and Polly angry, and when she had caught him at last, she vented her temper. When she returned to the honeysuckle window, her page looked quite spoiled, and though she wiped it off with copious tears, it never was clean and fair again. In her thoughts she always called it her "passion page."

Then there was another beautiful picture that she hated the sight of. It was the face, very noble and beautiful, of a great and famous soldier, which Polly found one day in a magazine of her father's. When she asked her mother if she might cut it out for her scrapbook, her mother said, "No; I thought I would propose to you to carry it over to the Corporal; he is sick, and both book and picture would interest him."

Polly turned away silently, and later in the day crossed the street with the book to the old soldier, but coveting the picture, she could not resist keeping it for herself. Some weeks after, when her mother came upon it pasted down in the scrapbook, she turned the saddest eyes on her little daughter and said, "Oh, Polly, Polly, beautiful pictures are not worth much if you don't do beautiful things. To have made a sacrifice for the old Corporal would have been worth a hundred pictures."

There was another dreadful page—upside down—done in stolen time, when Polly should have been studying.

But then, happily, came some hills of Beulah: some fair, sweet pages full of memories of quiet mornings in her mother's room when the sun streamed in at the honeysuckle window and filled the place with light and perfume. Her mother and Geoffrey had sat near Polly and filled the time with pleasant talk—for she and Geoffrey had long since forgiven each other the deluge of paste and its consequences. Indeed one of her pleasantest pages was one that followed hard upon it, containing a very ugly picture that Geoffrey had given her. In happy triumph, he had told her he'd traded a pocketful of marbles and a top for it, and though it was so ugly that it gave Polly a pang, she pasted it down with a smile and loved it—for Geoffrey's sake.

Polly had grown to be quite a big girl, and the May Day violets had come and gone several times before her scrapbook was finished. She chose a picture of a robin, dead in the snow, to appropriately mark its *finis.*

"I say, Polly," cried Geoffrey who sat at her table as she finished it, "this is your amen!"

"Yes," answered Polly, with the touch of gravity we all feel when we finish the smallest thing we have loved; and, bending over, she kissed Geoffrey and her mother. They were her best friends, and thus became part and parcel of her book of remembrance.

HUNTSVILLE, ALA.   [12 November 1879]

Household Decoration

By Flake White

Dr. Mason had finished his breakfast and, before going out among his patients, was taking his customary five-minute glance at the morning paper. His daughter, Rosamond, leaning on his shoulder with her blooming face pressed close to his cheek, was reading it with him according to *her* usual custom.

"See, Father," she cried excitedly, and pointing to an advertisement under the head of "Relics for Sale," read aloud, "Old table—brought over in the Mayflower—105 Constance Street."

Dr. Mason threw down his paper, laughed heartily and said, "Well, Mother, this Rosamond of ours is not losing her mania for 'household decoration,' evidently. Here is a paper full of foreign, political and fashion news—columns of it—and the only thing she sees worthy of note is the mention of an old table!"

"Never mind," answered Mrs. Mason placidly from her end of the table, "too much interest in the political might argue her strong-minded; too much in the fashions, flippant; as long as her fancy is homebound, she is safe. I don't object to a taste for old tables, myself."

"Neither does Father," said Rosamond saucily. "For just as soon as I get my hat, he is going to take me in his buggy to 105 Constance Street to see this one, and if it's what I want, he is going to let me buy it for our new library."

Two minutes later, Rosamond and her father were driving toward Constance Street, beyond which one of his patients was living. Dr. Mason dropped Rosamond at Number 105 and promised to call for her again in half an hour.

The house at whose door she knocked was the center of a block of tenement cottages, the most monotonous stretch of houses imaginable. A sort of contagion seemed to possess them. The gate of every one was off its hinges, and the bit of ground in front of each choked with rubbish; the windows were uniformly broken and unsightly, and in not one along the whole row was there so much as a single blooming plant to comfort or mark the place as home. It was easy to understand that they were the residences of factory hands who spent most of their time in the mills nearby. "Yet all the more need," Rosamond thought, "for these to be cheerful homes to come to after the noise and dust of the long days in the mills."

The knock was answered by a grave, not uncomely woman, whose appearance was much neater than the home warranted one to expect and who, in answer to Rosamond's quest, led the way into a small, dark front room in which stood the puritan table. Its merits were of a reserved sort that made it seem hardly out of place even in so poor a room, but its austere solidity made everything else about it look shabby and evanescent. The grave woman briefly told its history and price; and then excused herself from the room, leaving her daughter Rhoda to take her place.

Rhoda had come in behind her mother so softly that Rosamond had not seen her till now, and when looking up into her face, she saw to her astonishment that tears, great pellucid drops, were running unchecked down her cheeks.

The mother had been so composed and grave that she had seemed like the table, a bit of old still life preserved from the Pilgrims; and for a moment Rosamond was incredulous of the moved, tearful girl before her. But then in her impulsive way—quick to read feeling—she said, "You do not want to part with the table, do you?"

"It is the only pretty thing in the world we have," answered the girl briefly.

"Then indeed I won't take it," Rosamond responded impulsively.

"But you must," interrupted Rhoda, quickly brushing away her tears, "look there." And turning, she pointed to a darkened corner of the room where in an armchair, asleep, sat an old man, white, wasted and bent. "We have been *so* poor since Father was hurt in the mills two years ago. Our John isn't old enough to get good wages yet, and all we have, Mother and I make by lace cleaning and mending, which is *so* little, and oh, it will help us very much if you will buy the table."

"Very well," answered Rosamond, "only you must promise to come and see it, after I get home, or I shall think you have not forgiven me for taking it."

One bright afternoon a week or two later, Rosamond was in her gallery watering the plants that made it like a hanging garden, when the gate opened and Rhoda entered. As Rosamond met her on the steps, Rhoda shyly explained that she had been delivering some lace nearby when she remembered her promise to come and see her table in its new home.

Rosamond led her up through the fragrant flowers into the house, down a broad, cool hall and into a small room. It was an ideal woman's book room, quiet and beautiful, entering which one felt she had left behind the jarring discord of the world, and could now stop, take breath and gather strength before joining its turmoil again. The floors were dark and shining; the soft, pale brown walls were lined with low bookcases, generously filled with books on their lower shelves. On the upper shelves, vases, jars, screens, and a hundred pretty bits of rare porcelain and bronze made a broken frieze of gracious color along the middle wall. Opposite the door, on a rich crimson rug against the soft hued wall, stood Rhoda's table. On it lay a pretty litter of scattered books and flowers, and above it hung a picture from Longfellow's "Miles Standish."

"You see, now," said Rosamond, "why it was I wanted your pilgrim table? It suits our puritan picture so well. Have you ever read the story?"

"No" answered Rhoda, turning her attentive eyes from the lovely picture to Rosamond, and shaking her head.

"Then you shall read it—and from your own book, too," said Rosamond. "I have two copies, and this is yours." She put into her guest's hands a richly bound copy of the poem, bidding her when she read it, to remember the friend who had her table.

How Rhoda returned thanks and made her way home she did not know. She seemed in a dream of pleasant things until she awoke with a rude shock, reaching her own dark and dismal home. In all of her home there did not seem a spot sweet enough in which to lay her new treasure. She stood for a moment quite still in the center of the shabby little "front room," then with a movement of eager decision, laid aside her book and bonnet, and pushing a small table to the window, she climbed upon it and took down the soiled curtains and the old hat that had dutifully filled a broken pane through the past winter.

With a rag and a vessel of clean water, Rhoda's deft hands soon wiped the old panes until they allowed heaven's sweet daylight to shine through. When an hour later her mother came in to bring the father's supper, she found him awake listening to his child tell of her visit to Rosamond's beautiful home where "everything was clean and pretty colored, and so peaceful!"

The next day the curtains were washed and ironed and hung in their places, a clean white cover was laid over the well scoured table, and on this finally, at a pretty angle with the corners of the table, was laid the beautiful book. Rhoda looked at it with proud satisfaction, and running to her father's chair said, "Now, Daddy, you can get some idea of how pretty Miss Rosamond's place looked; only there was drawn up to *her* table, a great arm chair, as if someone had just been sitting there, and had gone away, saying, "God bless this place!"

"Daddy," she continued, kneeling beside him, you remember that old caned chair we've got, that's never had any bottom in it and which mother uses to hold up one end of her ironing board? Well, she says I may have it if I will put something else in its place, and please, Daddy, won't you make a bottom for it? I've heard you say you used to know how to bottom chairs long ago."

"Too long ago. I've forgotten how, Rhody," he replied, lifting his thin hand and looking sadly at his weak trembling fingers.

"But you will try, Daddy, if I get you the cane," pleaded Rhoda.

"Do you think I could?" the old man cried, with sudden energy, looking wistfully in his child's strong, hopeful face. Nobody else thought he could ever do anything again, but Rhoda might be right. He remembered how as a lad he had learned the simple trade, and given it up for better work. Now his weak hands might take it up again—if Rhoda thought so.

A week later, Dr. Mason's buggy once more put Rosamond down at 105 Constance Street, and going in she found a bright, clean room in place of the dark, cheerless one she had entered before. At the table with its clean cover and precious book, now like a little shrine, knelt Rhoda, watching her father who with much labor and neatness had at last finished bottoming her chair.

"Why, it's beautiful, simply beautiful!" cried Rosamond with timid enthusiasm. "Mother's got ever so many to be done, which I'm sure she will have you do."

"Daddy will be kept busy, I'm thinking," said Rhoda proudly as she led Rosamond to the door and showed her how clean and nice John had made the bit of yard.

"Yes, Father saw him at work," said Rosamond, "and told me about it, so I came to bring these packets of flower seeds to sow."

"The landlord saw him, too," answered Rhoda, taking the seed, "and had the broken gate and fence mended, and says he will do the same for any cottage in the row where they will clean the yard. And this evening, if he knocks off work in time, John's going to whitewash the fence."

John did get home in time to whitewash the fence, but since a neighbor's bedspread hanging over it interfered with his work, Rhoda ran over to ask the owner to take it off.

On the steps of the adjoining cottage, she found an old woman, the grandmother of a brood of little children, whom she tended while the father and mother worked in the mills. The neighbor readily rose to remove the spread, while Rhoda told her how they had cleaned up their yard and gutters, mended the fence, and how she was going to plant a beautiful garden. Rhoda shared with her some flower seed, thinking *she* might like to have a garden, too.

"Why, yes," said the woman, "Richard will clean up the place, I think. And little Mary here and I can plant and tend it. I lived in the country when I was young," she continued with an eager, backward glance, "and oh! the lilacs, the wallflowers, and the pinks that grew there! They could bloom again if I had a garden here," she said softly, looking absently at the rough, unkempt piece of ground, her mind peopling it with the flowers that had bloomed and gone to dust half a century before.

And little Mary—whose gardens were before her—stooped and began picking up the sticks and rubbish so that a new garden could begin. How it throve, and how many others began would take too long to tell. Rosamond had dropped a very little pebble in the water, but its circles widened out of sight.

We only know into what waters we drop the stone. We never know to what far and lovely shore the ripples may reach.

HUNTSVILLE, ALA.
[29 November 1882]

Courtesy of The Weeden House Museum

"Head of Steer"
after James Hart[1]
by
Howard Weeden[2]

---

[1] James McDougal Hart (1828-1901). An American painter known
for his idyllic landscapes, especially with cows.

[2] Inscribed on the original frame for this canvas: "Exhibited at Art
Loan in Nashville. It won first prize."

REDMOND O'HANLON

The Bag of Guineas
A True Story

In a retired district of Ireland, where the Mourne mountains make a broken panorama of wild hills and dells so green as to make the name of "Emerald Isle" no idle boast, many long years ago, my grandfather owned a little farm.

It was like many another farm in Ireland, growing by the grace of God rather than human industry, for its owner sowed and reaped but little, the whole profit of the farm arising from the lovely natural pastures in which it abounded where large numbers of cattle were raised, which the butchers from the neighboring towns would come every week to purchase.

It was a bright, pretty sight to see my Irish gentleman grandsire and a group of big, ruddy butchers in their rough, picturesque dress, walking up and down the boreen, or little lane, that ran between the pastures, examining the cattle. They made their trades with national volubility that broke the soft air with many a peal of rich laughter, as some Irish bull broke into my grandfather's pastures and made the weekly cattle trade as good as an old play.

The buyers gone, my grandfather would come into the house and throw the guineas they had paid him into my grandmother's lap who would tie them up in a little canvas bag then carry them to the old oaken chest and lock them away for safekeeping.

That was the division of labor in my grandfather's house; he made the money, and his wife took care of it.

Late one afternoon, he came in tired and muddy from a long day in the cattle yard, and emptying a great pocketful of guineas into grandmother's lap, said, "I've nearly sold out to-day. As tomorrow is Fair Day in Newry,[1] I must ride over and buy some fresh cattle. So let's have an early breakfast, good wife."

The next morning before the sun was up, Grandfather had mounted his stout little highland pony, and Grandmother, bringing his bag of gold pieces out to the gate, helped tie it safely to his saddlebow. He threw the end of his cloak closely over it—for his journey lay through a robber-haunted country—and rode briskly away.

---

[1] Newry. A seaport, urban district and market town of County Down in Northern Ireland.

It was a beautiful morning in spring, and the sun, rising above the mountain, turned the fresh green of the trees and shrubs into burnished gold and flushed the white hawthorns that bordered the road until their blossoms became roseate.

Grandfather was musing gratefully upon the beauty around him, when, raising his eyes, he saw through the network of tender young ash trees that fringed the road, on a little hillock above, a file of savage-looking men, mounted and armed, and coming down into the road.

Grandfather was a brave man and accustomed to fronting sudden perils, but his heart quailed at the sight. For, brave as it might be, there was not a heart in Ireland could unmoved meet Redmond O'Hanlon, Ireland's bandit-hero—a desperado with a price set on his head, a highway robber known to be fearless and believed to be invincible, who knew no law save want, no creed except courage, and who took a life as carelessly as he took a purse.

Grandfather had but a moment to think, for in an instant the robbers would be in the road; but he had Irish quickness and Presbyterian courage, and thus he muttered, "They may take my life. They are many to one, but O'Hanlon shan't have these guineas." So, spurring his pony to the side of the road where a great bush of hawthorn stood like a drift of snow, he leaned over and dropped the bag of gold into its fragrant bosom which received it and closed again white and calm above the secret entrusted to it.

Another moment and he was back into the road, facing O'Hanlon and his men.

"I know where you are going," said O'Hanlon harshly, disdaining any less abrupt introduction.

"Faith, and you are welcome," answered Grandfather gaily.

"A truce to your impudence," continued O'Hanlon. "It's Fair Day at Newry, and you are going to buy cattle. Come, give me the money you carry, quick!"

"I have no money with me," returned my grandfather steadily.

"You lie!" shouted the highwayman, and unsheathing his sword, lifted it with a swiftness that left my grandfather only time to instinctively throw up his arm to guard his face. The sword brandished high, struck the branch of a young ash that overhung the road, and descending with broken force, spent itself upon my grandfather's arm which dropped—broken and covered with blood.

The next instant O'Hanlon's sword was rattling into its sheath again. "There, take your life," he muttered scornfully. "I never strike a man twice." And with a touch of the picturesque chivalry that had dazzled the world with the romance of "thieves' honor," wheeled his horse, bade his men follow, and was soon out of sight.

Grandfather waited till the sound of their horses' hooves died away before he wiped the blood from his splashed face. Then he pulled his bag of guineas from the hawthorn bush and tying it as best he could to his saddlebow, rode slowly homeward.

Astonishment is a weak word to describe the feeling with which Grandmother looked up from her work and saw Grandfather at the gate already, all pale and blood-stained. Her hands shook with fear as she helped him off his horse and into the house.

"Thank God to see me at all, good wife," he said gravely, and then with a twinkle in his eye, continued, "I did not buy any cattle at Newry to-day because I didn't go there. I did my trading on the way with Redmond O'Hanlon, and I made a broken arm and my own bag of guineas out of him—and a most excellent trade it was, I think, all things considered!"

But my grandmother could not laugh. She could only say, "Thank God, Thank God!"

HUNTSVILLE, ALA.   FLAKE WHITE
[31 July 1878]

Advertisement from the Huntsville Weekly *Mercury*, 11 October 1893

Editorial Note

Howard Weeden visited Chicago's Columbian Exposition in September of 1893.[1]

---

[1] Huntsville Weekly *Democrat*, 20 September, 1893. Howard Weeden Collection (Huntsville-Madison County Public Library).

Chicago World's Fair 1893   Image courtesy of Paul V. Galvin Library

A COLUMBIAN DISCOVERY

BY MISS HOWARD WEEDEN

It was the last day of Miss Vanderlyn's visit to the World's Fair, and as far as the other members of her party were concerned, she was spending it alone.

They had found two weeks of sightseeing sufficiently exhausting to be glad of a quiet day in their hotel, while she continued to welcome the exertion and fatigue, since it enabled her to sleep at night, and to forget by day things she did not wish to remember. You see, in spite of her reputation for superb indifference in love affairs, Miss Vanderlyn had managed to get at last a wounded heart herself, and had brought it to the Fair for cure, hoping that concentrated and cold-blooded study of painted men in the art galleries would enable her to forget real ones, and the mysteries of technique prove absorbing enough to supplant those of sentiment.

She had carried out her programme with punctilious vigor, and the last day of her visit found her still at work, studying the pictures with unnatural severity and annotating her catalogue with dismal determination. She entered the Holland gallery at high noon, and was about to take the only available resting place she saw—a seat at the end of a crowded bench—when the lady next to her rose and said, impersonally, "Let me give you more room. I am just leaving to keep an appointment at this hour in another gallery, and my little girl here is too tired to go with me. I am sure she will be safe near you for five minutes."

The child, a pretty little thing of six or seven years, lay back upon the seat in the nerveless attitude peculiar to sightseer's fatigue, and watched her mother drown herself in the crowd, without an effort to follow her. She turned a look of appeal upon Miss Vanderlyn, however, and said, plaintively, "This horrid old Fair! I wish I was at home."

Miss Vanderlyn frowned as she turned a cold glance upon the little speaker, wondering why fate had interrupted her last day at the Fair by committing, for even five minutes, a troublesome child to her care, but her eyes met a face so lovely, and so wearied, that she changed her mind about not replying, and asked her instead why she did not like the Fair.

"Because it's such a tired place," replied the child, "and there's not room enough. At home I'm never tired until night, and there's plenty of room for just me and Mamma and Uncle and Mammy, and the servants, you know. Mammy did not want me to come to the Fair; she said I'd get lost, and now I am. Everything gets lost here. I've bought a souvenir every day to take home to Mammy, and I have lost them all—a Turkish sword, a photograph of Mister Buffalo Bill, a glass walking stick and an inkstand. But perhaps, as Mammy can't write, she won't mind about the inkstand.

"Aunt Judy is our cook; she said if I did not look out, I wouldn't get any beaten biscuit here, and I haven't."

Miss Vanderlyn looked curiously at the little speaker, wondering idly at what place in the South her steadfast, homesick young heart was anchored, then, glancing at her watch and seeing that the five minutes were nearly spent, said, "Your mother will soon be back now." She carefully left her watch open on her knee to imply her value of the time that was being wasted.

Her reproach, however, failed to pierce the child's home-haunted mood, and she went on presently, with her eyes fixed smilingly on Mrs. Roosenbooms' garlands hanging on the opposite wall. "Just see those roses! They grow like that over all our galleries at home, bushels and bushels of them, and Uncle and I pelt each other with them till there's a carpet of leaves on the floor. And, once he sent a box of them to the lady he loved, who lives where it is cold and many roses do not grow. She wrote him a letter, and he carried it in his pocket, and read it, and read it, even when nobody saw him (but they did)."

Miss Vanderlyn did not raise her eyes to the child's, but kept them standing fastly on the watch, and, if she saw another five minutes slipping away, she did not mention it, so there was a little pause until the child said again, "I saw a splendid picture in one of the other rooms, of an old man with long, long fingernails, who looked just like our doctor at home. That was the reason why so many people were always standing around it. Ah," she continued, with a gesture of eloquent retrospection, "when he puts his hands on his knees and looks at you that way, you may as well put out your tongue, and call Mamma—you've got medicine to take!"

"I hope," said Miss Vanderlyn, lifting her eyes from her watch with a brilliant smile, "I hope, for the sake of the joke, that his name is Doctor Renan."

"No," said the child, with a joyous laugh, delighted to have at last brought a smile to the beautiful grave face beside her. "His name is not 'Renan.' You'll have to guess again!"

Miss Vanderlyn's watch ticked off a great many more five minutes in time to the endless domestic anecdotes, and still the little one's mother did not return. In some way, however, her hard artistic studies had come suddenly to seem so small and dismal beside the child's simple realities that her impatience to return to them had visibly declined, and it was the child herself, at last, who proposed that, now that she was rested, it might be a good plan to make their way through the Galleries, in doing which Miss Vanderlyn could look at the pictures, and she could look for her mother.

They found the journey no easy matter, with the heat and crowd increasing every moment, and Miss Vanderlyn gave herself so entirely to the duty of taking care of her charge that there would have been little attention given the pictures except when the choice of stopping before one was sometimes made by the child herself, if it happened to have the delightful and inestimable merit of reminding her of something belonging to home.

"The Good Brother," for instance, she was charmed to look at for awhile, because she said it was very like a little boy she often saw at home, "sitting just that way on his mother's steps, while his sister stood in front of him and waited for some of his orange, which he would not give her."

"We have plenty of oranges," she went on with aimless relevancy, "when we go to our place in

Florida, and once Uncle sent some to that same lady he loved and she wrote him another letter, and you had to cough every time you went into a room where he was, to keep from catching him reading it—forever and forever!"

Image courtesy of Paul V. Galvin Library

"The Good Brother"
Eugen von Blaas (1843-1931)

She could not pass the "Empty Saddle" either, but must needs stop for the joy of telling how the horse reminded her of Uncle's pretty mare. "He named her after that lady," said the child, "and he would pat her neck and call her 'Alice,' so softly no one could hear him, only me, and Mamma told me not to listen."

"I must stop here a moment," said Miss Vanderlyn, when they reached the Loan Collection and found themselves before the "Dead Toreador."

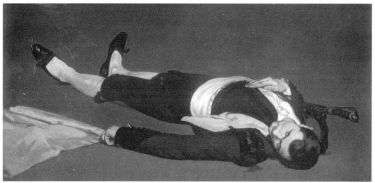

"The Dead Toreador"
Edouard Manet (1832-1883)

"I want to study this picture well again, and after that, we must not stop to look at any more pictures until your mother is found."

There was a moment's silence as the two paused before the pathetic figure stretched out in its last pale sleep, and Miss Vanderlyn had time to feel glad, with a strange gladness, that the happy child would find no reminder in such a tragedy of anything that belonged to the sunny life of which she seemed so free to talk, but presently there was a tighter clasp of the little hand, and a closer nestling to her side, and then the child said very gravely, "That's just the way Uncle looked when I used to creep into his room, and stand at the head of his bed, and he so ill! His hand was always on his breast, that way, where he used to keep that lady's letters, before she took them back and broke his heart. Mamma said 'twas that 'twas killing him. And that is the way he looked, white, and with his hand forever on his breast."

Miss Vanderlyn dropped her catalogue and pencil, and with a low, inarticulate cry, caught the child close to her.

"Tell me the rest, little girl," she cried, "Oh, tell me, did he get well again?"

"Why, of course he did," the child replied, with a sudden return to carelessness. "'Twas him Mamma went to meet, and here they are now! Mamma," she cried, and the next moment was in her mother's arms, and the man was looking at Miss Vanderlyn.

"Alice!" he said.

His face was white as the Toreador's, and love and doubt were fighting hard for mastery. Miss Vanderlyn, the imperious, was trembling like a leaf. She laid both hands on his arm, and raised a quivering face to his, and said, "You have been ill, and did not let me know! Oh, I'm so sorry—for everything! I never knew, until today, how much you cared, or how much I—cared." She ended very low, but he bent his head to listen, and if he touched her cheek with his lips, who saw him in the crowd?

[4 April 1894]

Christmas

Dubuffe

The Widow's Mite
Mark 12:42

Self-Denial

It was a bright winter's evening—so balmy as hardly to seem like the week before Christmas. Old Joseph Harper stood leaning against his door, talking to the minister, both too much interested in their conversation to notice the softness of the air or the beauty of the sunset.

"Self-denial indeed!" said old Joseph, taking his pipe from his mouth. "I don't believe in it as a part of *religion*. It is enacted often enough, but there's always some selfishness behind it."

"Your words prove this much, my friend," said the minister, looking at him regretfully, "that you have never practiced it yourself." With a kind goodbye to Edward Harper, the old man's grandson, who stood near his grandfather in the doorway, the minister took his leave.

"Why, Grandfather," said Edward, looking up earnestly, "we Sunday School children practice some self-denial almost every week."

"Yes," said his grandfather, "you buy as much candy as you want with your money, and what's *left* you carry to your teacher; but did you or any other chap like you ever *deny* yourselves to give the money?"

Edward was silent. He felt that his grandfather was much too bitter and severe, yet when he thought it over, the boy was less satisfied that their giving was always pure.

A moment after, they both left the door and drew up to the blazing fire. Between Edward's thoughtfulness and Mr. Harper's moodiness, there was silence until Edward said, "Grandfather, didn't you tell the man that brought the wood to come in the morning and cut it up?"

"Yes," he replied.

"Will you give me the money you promised him if I will cut it?"

"Yes, but I thought you said you didn't have time," his grandfather said.

"Well, we boys were all going over to the old field before school and have a great bonfire; but as you say the wood can't wait till evening, I will give up the bonfire and commence on it before school."

To leave his bed next morning before sunrise would have been an effort even with the glorious bonfire in view. But to leave it that he might spend the next three hours cutting wood and storing it away, was an effort so great that self-comfort might have proven stronger than the promised half dollar. Yet the longing to carry a larger offering than usual on the Sabbath of Christmas week became strong enough to overpower his other emotions.

"Pretty cold morning, Edward," said Mr. Harper, as they sat down to breakfast.

"Yes, sir," he replied, "the coldest of the season."

"The boys didn't feel it around the bon-fire, I reckon," Mr. Harper continued.

"No, sir, nor I over my good exercise," Edward said smiling.

Mr. Harper looked at him inquiringly for a moment. Woodcutting, he knew, was a peculiar aversion of Edward's, and he was a little curious to know what had moved him to employ himself upon it, when he really wished to be elsewhere.

It was Friday, and when school was out the boys' shouts rung through the playground in honor of the next week's holiday.

"Just waiting for you, Edward," exclaimed three boys whom he found standing near his door.

The largest boy of the group continued, "Father says the fireworks have come at the store and if we come up after school he will have them open and will sell us the kind we want, cheap. With what we three have got, and the half you showed us this morning, we can buy enough to send up a splendid welcome to Christmas holiday tonight on the common. Now come, Edward, nobody knows the fireworks are here, and we will astonish the other boys so."

To go up to the store and see the beautiful Christmas things, and then to be one to enjoy the fun on the common, was a most delightful anticipation; and though his face had lighted up a moment, Edward said nothing, and his brow clouded as he moved off, the only silent one in the chattering group. The boys looked about the gay store for some time, and then gathered around the fireworks. "I am very sorry, boys," said Edward hesitatingly, "but I can't give my half dollar."

"You haven't spent it!" said the boys.

"No," he replied.

"Well, what is there that you would rather spend it for than these?"

"I am not going to buy anything with it," and before they could reply, or before they could see the tears that filled his eyes, Edward was gone. In his haste, he failed to notice a gentleman standing in the doorway.

"I am glad I left," said Edward to himself, as he ran down the street. "I couldn't have stood the temptation much longer."

That evening, after their rather silent tea, Edward and his grandfather took their seats near the fire. There being no more lessons for a week, Edward took down his Bible to find a verse for Sunday. As he opened it, his eye fell upon the verse, "the Lord loveth a cheerful giver." Unconsciously he read it aloud.

"Why didn't you show yourself a cheerful giver this evening?" his grandfather said, looking at him keenly.

"Because I kept my gift to show myself one on Sunday," Edward replied, and then said, "How did you know any thing about it, Grandfather?"

"I was standing near you and heard the whole affair," he replied, "and was somewhat mortified at your apparent want of liberality. What is it you are hoarding that money for?"

"I thought," Edward said, "after what the minister told us about self-denial the other evening, that very few of my contributions to the Sunday School had been fruits of sacrifice, and though I had the ten cents you gave me to carry, I thought I would try and offer on Christmas Sabbath a real self-denial."

"It was a double denial that I hadn't looked for," he continued after a short pause, in which the bursting of a rocket and the shout of voices reached his ear from the common. "To cut up the wood was all I had expected, but," his lips quivering slightly, "giving up fireworks is the harder."

"I have found it!" Mr. Harper said, as he looked earnestly at the boy's thoughtful face. "And if every feature in this religion, which the minister says to learn we must become as little children, be as beautiful as this, then I should like to be a Christian."

Every child is a minister, even in a little way, and giving of a piece of Sunday School money may be made as beautiful a sermon as that of the often read "widow's mite."

HUNTSVILLE, ALA.   FLAKE WHITE
[30 August 1866]

KING GOOD-GOLD
AND LITTLE GOOD-WILL

The Two Christmas Fairies

Perhaps the moon knew it was Christmas Eve. Certainly she seemed to shine down upon the world with unwonted lustre and tenderness, for even the lonely mountain passes, with their dismal firs and ghostly ravines, lay smiling and tranquil in her light; and the very owls held their breath, as if such a night were meant for nightingales alone.

Winding through one of these passes a road lay white and smooth in its covering of deep snow, over which two most remarkable looking travellers were taking their way.

A sleigh, swelling with soft furs and purring comfortably along, contained the most notable looking of the two. He was a diminutive person— as well as could be judged for he was enveloped by luxuriant robes of ermine and green velvet which gave forth a dainty perfume whenever the wind stirred them. A shower of golden hair fell about his fair face from under a splendid crown that set the royal seal upon this personage. For he was none other than his majesty King Good-Gold, on his way to the world laden with Christmas tokens that jingled a golden, subdued music whenever a sudden declivity in the pass sent the sleigh gliding down the road with accelerated speed.

Just behind the sleigh followed the other traveller, Little Good-Will, a lithe figure clad in sober brown, and without ornament save a sprig of red-berried holly that flamed in his cap. He seemed to have no connection with the royal sleigh, whose shadow he kept studiously between them. He threw no more shadow himself than if he had been transparent, and danced along with so light, fantastic and weird-like abandon, that one would have proclaimed him a russet ghost. But such hobgoblins are said to fear the sound of bells, and whenever, in the pauses of the wind, the Christmas chimes from the churches below would reach him, Little Good-Will would burst into an ecstacy of song so loud and clear that the rocks themselves would answer back.

No sound was heard from the sleigh save the jingle of its gold.

The wild road was passed at last and the first house of a city's straggling suburbs was reached. It was poor and low and escaped the notice of King Good-Gold, who drove swiftly past; but Little

Good-Will opened the door and entered. A poor, begrimed miner sat before a fire, with wife and children gathered about him, and all bending anxiously forward while the father slowly counted on his knee a small handful of beggarly coins.

"Fortune is unkind, indeed, to pay my hard labor so meagrely," he was muttering, when a sudden draft of cold air made them all look up, and Little Good-Will, with a merry "Peace and Good Will" carol still lingering on his lips, bounded into their midst.

"Such a warm fire as you always do keep, Mike!" he exclaimed, bending over it till his holly berries caught its glow. "And you escaped unhurt from the accident in the mine a few days since!" He continued, "And Nannie is well again!" touching her rosy cheeks. "Well, you have got a great deal to be thankful for."

"Yes, yes," cried Mike, drawing Nannie to him, and looking more forgivingly at the little pile of coins, "and thank you for reminding us of it."

With a quick farewell, Good-Will was gone speeding across the snow and singing as he went, while the miner forgetting his pitiful wages returned with a new light in his face to the fire and there counted his blessings.

King Good-Gold was just leaving the next house when Good-Will reached it and, entering a warm brilliant room, found a group of children noisily contending over the handful of gold which his majesty had thrown in among them. There was less merriment than ill humor, for the little ones found the larger children got the lion's share of sparkling coins. But suddenly a voice singing a sweet chant of Christmas peace burst with a draft of snow-laden air into the room and ushered in Good-Will, around whom the children hastily rose and gathered in reverence.

"That gust of wind is just a taste of the weather without," he said, "and it isn't the same fun looking for money out in the snow as it is on this ruddy fire-lighted carpet. As I crossed a mountain tonight, I came upon a little boy, who with tear-blinded eyes was searching for one lost coin—smaller than the smallest piece among you. The tiny coin seemed very large to him, though, for it was his first wages that he was proudly taking home. I got down beside him to help search—for, bless you, I had no more money to give him. Presently I found the coin in a snowdrift and sent him home happy." In telling this story, Good-Will burst into a song like heartbeats set to music.

The next house at which Good-Will stopped, although poor and humble, had also had a hasty visit from King Good-Gold. Good-Will entered the low door which his majesty had opened wide enough to toss in a little coin of gold which still lay upon the floor unheeded by the girl sitting over a dull fire. "Gold will not bring Father back," she said, "and they tell me he was killed in the mine, and I am alone, alone!"

"What a sorrowful tale to be telling Christmas Eve!" Good-Will cried, kneeling to stir the fire into a bright glow. "I can tell a story that will make you feel better. Last night was such a stormy night that Mother Charity and I could not sleep for the wind, and sitting over our fire near the morning, we heard a cry for help. Mother held a rush light at the window, while I ran out to a nearby ravine. The day before a bridge had spanned it, but the storm had taken all of the bridge away—save one log. On the other side a perishing traveller cried for help. There was no way for me to cross the dizzy place but on the uncertain log, which I did, and with words of encouragement I convinced the poor, belated miner to come back with me in the same way. It was your father rescued from the mine, as your joyful tears show you have already guessed, Margarite. A good rest beside Mother Charity's warm fire has renewed him for the journey home and he will soon be with you. Now I must go—for when one makes a pilgrimage of kind words and deeds around the world, there is no time to spare!"

Margarite, with happy face, watched him from the door as he went on his way to cheer other waiting hearts. His "Peace and Good Will" carol swelled upon the wind, mingling with the peal of Christmas bells.

HUNTSVILLE, ALA.
[22 December 1869]

The Two Fortunes

There lived once upon a time, long gone by, a poor woodcutter, who had two sons, between whom, when he came to die, he divided all he had. This consisted of a donkey, upon which he carried his wood and the ax with which he cut it. The cottage where they lived did not belong to him; so, when he was dead, the two boys—finding themselves homeless as well as fatherless—bade farewell to the old place, and one morning toward the Christmas of the year started off into the world together.

Their way lay along a narrow, rarely travelled forest road, whose loneliness was unbroken save by the continued chatter of Fritz, who, mounted upon old White Foot, poured from his soft elevation a querulous strain of complaints against the fate that rendered them so poor and so friendless.

"How shall we get up through the world?" he asked of Carl, who strode along beside him with ax a-shoulder and head meditatively bent.

"You are to ride through on White Foot," he answered, "and I am to cut my way through."

So the day passed, and their separation was at

hand in this wise: the narrow road had brought them to a bridge that spanned a mountain stream all swollen by the storm of the night before. In its violence, the wind had thrown a tree across the path and just in front of the bridge. White Foot stopped short and shook his ears.

Fritz shook his head and then said lazily, "I'll ride down the stream till I find another way across." And turning White Foot's head, he followed the lead of the foaming stream.

A moment more and Carl's ax was down from his shoulder, and the forest was soon throbbing with its strokes, as he cut the tree away from the path. The young woodsman was just finishing his work, when a travelling carriage came up to the scene of his labors, and the occupant, a personage of apparent importance, got out and questioned Carl as to what he was doing.

"My brother and I were the first travellers to reach the bridge since the storm," Carl answered, "and he, having a donkey, rode round. I, having none, was obliged to cut my way through."

"Do you not perceive, my young friend, that you have cut my way through, too?" said the stranger. "How may I repay you?"

"By passing over first, Sir," replied the boy, raising his cap and stepping aside, while the gentleman, with a tribute of courtesy to courtesy, raised his own hat, and stepping into the carriage, thundered across the bridge and was soon out of sight.

Carl now stopped to rest awhile, then gathering up a bundle of the wood he had cut, swung it across his back and took his way over the bridge. As night approached, it was with gratitude that he saw a light before him and soon reached the kind shelter of an old miner's cottage.

The miner had been sick for several days, and was shivering over a low fire, upon which Carl at once threw a part of his wood and soon had it blazing brightly. In time, the two seemed to forget the storm that howled without, and that was now accompanied with fast descending snow.

As the night wore on, it grew colder, but at last the wind died away so that Carl and the old miner fell asleep. Again and again they awoke and piled on the wood, and the night became still as death. At last the wood was all burned and Carl rose and tried to open first the door and then the frail windows, but could not. The horrible truth then dawned upon them that they were buried in a snowdrift.

There was no time to lose, and taking his ax in hand, Carl climbed into the roof of the hut and soon had an opening cut, through which a blinding shower of snow fell. He cut still farther through their frozen burial sheet, and presently found daylight. Carl climbed out and making way to a cluster of miner's huts situated in the rocks above the drift, soon found plenty of willing hands to unbury the old miner and his home.

Carl, finding it impossible to continue his journey until the severity of stormy days was over, remained with his grateful old friend. He spent most of his idle time, as was his habit, carving in wood with his faithful knife such figures as turned in his brain and daintily came from his hand. With thoughts on the holy season near, he now busied himself working a piece of white wood into a cross enwreathed with holly, which was a marvel of grace. By the time it was finished he bade goodbye to the miner whom he had rescued, and started on his journey again.

Fortunately his travel was short, for on Christmas Eve he reached the city of his destination, which was bright with people whose faces glowed with the coming of Christmas. To poor ragged Carl, hungry and friendless, this place seemed lovelier than the country—for there was no wood to gather and cut. The shop windows were so rich in beautiful things that he dared not show his modest carving. But late that windy Christmas Eve as he stood, ax on his shoulder, cross in his hand, sheltering himself in a doorway, the door opened and a gentleman came out. Seeing the cross in Carl's hand, the man asked to look at it. Looking more closely at Carl he exclaimed, "I thought so! You are the little friend who cut our way over the bridge."

And sure enough it was the traveller from the bridge who now drew Carl into a room bright with fire and lights and books and marvelous white statues.

"Cutting your way still?" he queried. But Carl paused in silence before the dazzling stone statues. "Only cutting it in a finer way now!" continued the man, still examining Carl's cross and holly wreath.

"After looking at these grand marbles, it seems fit only to be thrown in the fire," the boy said apologetically. "But I shall do better some day."

"To be sure you will," said the master, laughing at the boy's calm manner. "You would cut your way through, no doubt, without help, but it will be my pleasure to help you. I am a sculptor; these marbles are my work, and from tonight you are my pupil."

Carl did not leave the sculptor again, and when he woke next morning under the kind shelter of his roof, he thought the joy bells must be ringing his own good fortune, too, as they pealed their "Peace and Good Will" on the Christmas air.

In the years that followed, Carl won his way bravely and patiently into honor and happiness. Occasionally, he heard from Fritz, who was always poor and lazy, and ready to receive the help his brother so gladly gave him.

White Foot had done all he could for Fritz, but unfortunately, the two lacked perseverance enough to "cut their way through."

HUNTSVILLE, ALA   FLAKE WHITE
[9 December 1874]

THE SCARLET CLOAK

A Christmas Story

The pale uncertain dawn of a bleak winter morning crept slowly over the mountains and filled the valleys with ghastly light. Through the rock-sheltered nook where a little hamlet stood, the light softly entered one of its modest huts. There it fell upon a wretched pallet and awoke the little sleeper.

"Morning," said Rolf, shivering, "and time to be on my journey." Rising, he dressed himself quickly in clothes whose rags and patches and pitiful scantiness even the mountain light could not conceal. Then with a radiant smile he eagerly turned back his pillow and took out a new and carefully folded scarlet cloak, which he fastened with a dainty air over his ragged jacket. Last of all, he drew forth a covered violin, strapped it across his shoulder, and went out into the raw morning.

It was the day before Christmas, and Rolf was ready to start on a tour through the great cities, where he hoped something more substantial than praise might be given for his music that the simple village children thought so beautiful.

For some months Rolf's every cent had been laid aside for preparatory investment. He must needs have a cloak, and—happy thought!—it should be red to cover daintily the ragged clothes he could not better, and bright to attract the otherwise indifferent public. "Red is the color that will help sound," he argued to himself. So now, as he trudged through the gray, melancholy dawn, the cloak seemed to glow like something living, and Rolf's heart broke out into an echoing carol—as we sometimes see a robin's crimson throat throb into music.

The journey was not a lonely one. Some travellers, with the coming Christmas shining in their faces, passed to and fro along the road, and scarcely one but gave a smile to the gaily cloaked musician—tho' they gave nothing more, not even when seeing him at wayside inns. Rolf took up his violin and played his best for them, often so wearily that it was as if his own breath performed upon the strings.

Toward noon, he was standing at the door of a glaring forge, holding the horse of a fur-cloaked gentleman, who had alighted to warm himself. Then two very different-looking travellers stopped for the same purpose—a blind old man, led by a little girl, whose poor thin garments were patched and worn with womanly neatness. As they passed at the door, she touched Rolf's gay cloak and then in guileless eagerness, and simple eloquence, told her grandfather what a beautiful cloak their little fellow-traveller wore! How it was soft and warm, and shone like the forge fire. The old man turned his sightless eyes upon her, and compassionately caressed the little arm upon which he leaned.

The bright smile with which Rolf heard his cloak admired presently faded away. After a moment's thought, he unfastened it, called the child nearer, and threw it on her shoulders in place of the old dingy black one she wore. This, he wrapped about himself, saying, with a laugh, that "it was good enough for a boy, while the scarlet one would look wondrous well upon her at the fair." Then he bade her go in to the fire. When the fur-cloaked gentleman came out to mount his horse, he dropped a coin in Rolf's hand before riding away.

So the day wore along, and sometime after nightfall, Rolf reached his destination, a great noisy, friendless city. With his single coin spent for a lodging, he was soon fast asleep.

When he awoke, a bright Christmas sun and a babel of Christmas noises were flooding the great city, and it seemed to poor Rolf that all the jarring music of the world had collected there. Men, boys and girls, with harps, violins and guitars, crowded the streets, and there seemed not a crevice in the din in which he could creep with his music.

All day he wandered unnoticed, never daring to add one of his soft melodies to the loud medley. And no one bade him play, for they did not know his touch was fine—he was so small and ragged! But never mind; he was glad he had given his pretty cloak away, and Rolf paused a moment to think of the little child he had gladdened with it, hardly conscious in the universal din, that he had paused near a group of musicians, who were playing lustily beneath the window of a fine and stately house. Its door was presently opened, and a richly dressed man threw a handful of coins to them and bade them "be off with your discordant music." He was closing the door again, when he caught sight of Rolf.

"I think we were fellow travellers yesterday," he said, eyeing him intently. "Did I not see you at the wayside forge, exchange scarlet feathers for those black ones? Come in, and let us see if they carry any music under them."

So Rolf followed him into a firelit room, warm and rich with curtains and carpets, and crowded with a piano, various other musical instruments, and piles of books and scattered music. The master bade him warm his cold hands, and then invited him to play. So Rolf played his little fiddle—timidly at first, but bolder by degrees— one of his mountain melodies that was full of echoes and all such sounds.

When he ceased, the master was wiping away a tear. "I was born among the mountains," he said, "and feel deeply the sweetness of your music; I do not see why we should part. I, too, am a musician, and we can serve each other. Your gentle deed touched me yesterday as your scarlet cloak never would have done, and with so true a heart to guide your hand, you will not be long in drawing the world to hear your music."

And thus it was—that the scarlet cloak made young Rolf's fortune in a way he had never dreamed.

HUNTSVILLE, ALA.   FLAKE WHITE
[20 December 1871 and
23 December 1896]

An Alpine Lad's Story

An Alpine Lad's Story

Wailing wind swept through a mountain glen, stern and desolate in its gray rocks and sobbing pines. The only sign of life was a thin wreath of smoke that curled up toward the evening sky from a cottage hearthstone where a poor widow sat with her busy wheel beside her. It ceased its hum for a moment as she paused to receive Reuben's farewell kiss and Merry Christmas. He left her to join a waiting comrade with whom he was going to spend the holiday.

"It is getting late," said Mark, as Reuben came out into the deepening twilight. Both leaped across the torrent that plowed down the pass, and struck up the rugged mountain path. It was fast getting colder, too, and great flakes of snow floated down through the grey air and mingled with the whirl of dead leaves.

The two boys gathered their coats about them closely and drew nearer together as they made their rapid way like young chamois up the road, anticipating pleasant comforts awaiting them at

Mark's home: the faces of the children, watching at the bright window for them; the heap of glowing logs on the broad, shining hearth; the smoking supper, the apples, the roasted chestnuts; the merry games prolonged until Christmas day. These humble Christmas-eve pleasures made amusing chatter for the boys, though the wind blew blindingly in their faces, and made them pause sometimes and bend before it till its fury was passed.

Their journey was half accomplished, when suddenly they were stopped in the road by a man slowly leading a horse. The animal had become so lame that, though nearly broken down himself, the man had been obliged to dismount and was now attempting to make his way on foot. They could see through the darkness that he was feeble from age and weariness, and travel-stained as if from a long journey. His weak voice shook as he asked how far before he reached the next house.

"Some distance, sir," said Reuben. "My mother's cottage is the nearest."

"It is a bitter night," said the old man, shivering. "I am afraid I will never reach it alone."

How bright in Reuben's mind shone the Christmas fire at Mark's. How musically the children's voices seemed to rise above the wind. But how worn and wearied the old man looked, bent before the wind, and white with the falling snow. Reuben slowly unlinked his arm from

Mark's, saying softly, "Good night and Merry Christmas. I must go back." And taking the bridle from the old man's hand, he led the way down the pass.

With the lame horse, the feebleness of the old man, and the fury of the wind, they were a long time in reaching the cottage. Once safely there, new logs were piled on the fire, and warm clothes and a frugal supper were found for the stranger. Reuben, giving him his bed, threw himself down upon the pallet before the fire and made Christmas pictures in the coals till his weariness rubbed them out and he was fast asleep.

This first severe storm of the winter was only the forerunner of the most terrible tempests the people of this unhappy pass had ever known. Storm after storm of wild wind and cruel snow raged down the defiles, leaving uprooted trees and buried houses in its wake. To add to this evil, food was scarce, and sickness and famine came on. Few suffered more than poor Reuben and his mother, until, overpowered at last by want and anxiety, her grave was made beside her husband's, and Reuben was left alone—almost literally alone in the valley now, for, driven by sickness and famine, nearly all the inhabitants had left the mountains and gone to seek help in the cities below.

So early one morning, after a night of storm, Reuben closed the old hut door for the last time. Peering through his blinding tears, he looked at the lonely graves under the cedars, then turned down the mountain and set out for the world.

Slowly and hopelessly he made his way down, till at last he reached a city whose cleanliness and order, and whose whirl of business almost seemed a dream after the waste and storm desolation of his mountain home. But its streets were full of sufferers like himself, and men turned deaf ears to his tale that sounded to them only a repetition of what they had heard before. At last, in despair, he threw himself down to rest upon a low, broad stone step and wept as if his heart would break.

Presently a hand was laid on his shoulder and rising, the boy was about to stand aside for a man to enter his house. "Why, Reuben, my boy, have you forgotten the old man whose journey over the mountain caused you such a self-denial once? Come into the fire and let me show you that I have not."

So, at last poor Reuben was housed and shielded from storm and want. God had seen his sacrificial bread cast upon the waters. From his comfortable home henceforth he went to and fro to hearty earnest work, compelled no more to seek the trials of the old mountain life. Yet sometimes when the early violets draped the hills like blue mist, he would make a spring journey to where they were blooming peacefully over the graves beneath the cedars.

HUNTSVILLE, ALA.   [13 August 1868]

A Christmas Card

By Flake White

Dorothy Herman laid off her faded shawl and hood, and kneeling down on the hearth, warmed her cold hands by its small fire. She had just come in from the little picture shop around the corner, where she had left some hollywood panels which the old art dealer had asked her to decorate. Though he had not paid her much for her pretty work, she still had brought away a peculiarly bright and eager look, which even her dismal room was unable to dispel. She was still thinking of the little shop, bright in all its holiday bravery, and most of all, of its many Christmas cards, and the happy people who were busy buying them.

"What a beautiful way to send good will to men," Dorothy thought, "with a lovely card bearing reverent text for Him who loved us, and a radiant greeting for those whom we love." She wished from the bottom of her heart that she might send a card to someone. But she was quite alone in the world, and there was no one she had a right to love.

Less than a year before she had come from the old world with her father, who had been tempted to America by his brother, a musician who had left their homeland for a great city in the new world. So, here motherless Dorothy and her father had sought him—but in vain, for her uncle had changed his residence. Then, only a week after their arrival, Dorothy's father succumbed to a fever that he had contracted on board the ship, and thus travelled to a still newer world. Dorothy was left alone.

Quite friendless and penniless, her condition would have been desperate had her landlady not offered her a continued home in her house, in return for her services in teaching her children, and such means as Dorothy earned with her brush. Thus was her lonely and laborious life as her first Christmas in the new world rolled round. A more morbid nature than Dorothy's might have thought this a bitter moment, as she knelt before her meagre fire, realizing she had not a single friend with whom to share the joy of sending or receiving a card.

But Dorothy's creed about Christmas cards was a little broader than simply sending them to loved ones. She imagined that such charmed greetings might also be sent to lonely people. Not people to whom we owe a card—not people who expect a card from us, or with whom we might be more popular if we so distinguished them, but simply lonely souls who might enjoy a sign of earth's cheer and heaven's blessing.

Dorothy hastily thought over the members of her landlady's household (her little world) and the person least likely to be remembered was the lonely old woman universally called "the Madam" who had boarded there for a long time. She had an air of dignity about her, even though she had neither money, home, nor friends.

When the lady's rheumatism was very bad, Dorothy sometimes carried her meals to her room and felt her heart bleed for this one whose loneliness was so much sadder than her own because it was so much older! Here, then, was someone she might remember at Christmas. Having settled that, there was only the card to prepare. Rising from her knees on the hearth with an air of cheerful assurance, Dorothy lit the lamp on her little painting table.

From that hour until Christmas, she gave every spare moment to her happy work, and spun a web from the heart of her own lonely life. The design represented an aged figure, like an image of the old year, seated near a dim fire, poor and alone. Softly outlined against the gloom was an angel bending, bathing her in a smile so tender and a radiance so rich that the poverty of the figure was forgotten in the heavenly compensation.

Beneath it, in letters of solemn splendor that seemed to light up with holy fire ran the legend: "All things are yours."

On Christmas morning, Dorothy's precious card waited to be delivered. She rose while it was yet dark and, shivering as she dressed, planned how she would creep to the Madam's room, softly slip the card under it, and lightly, so lightly, run away.

Just then her own door opened and her distressed landlady, out of breath, begged, "Please come downstairs and help me. Every servant is late—as usual on Christmas!"

So Dorothy bustled after her and was busy getting the lagging holiday wheels in motion and had not a moment in which to think of her card until breakfast was served. Then learning that Madam's rheumatism would keep her in her room, Dorothy put her breakfast on a tray and started upstairs. On the way she stopped for the card and placed it beside the plate.

It was an even better way of delivering it than the other, for when Dorothy entered the room and saw the poor Madam sitting so cold and forlorn beside her wretched fire, she felt a sudden rush of added pity. She stooped shyly in her quaint, foreign fashion and kissed the old lady softly on the cheek. Then putting the tray and card in her lap, Dorothy hastened to stir the dying fire. Laying a warmer shawl about the aching shoulders, she pulled back the dingy curtain, which, letting in a flood of sunshine, lit up the card to the Madam's wondering eyes!

"And just to think," said Madam after awhile, "I never began a day feeling so poor, so cold and so aching! I forgot my riches for a moment," and she turned from Dorothy's happy face to her card again.

Later in the morning, the tired landlady dropped in to see her old boarder who eagerly showed the card, asking her what it seemed to say to *her*. The landlady looked at it a long time, her anxious face softening as she said, "Well, I suppose it means to remind me that something good is safely laid away—out of sight—for those who, like me, don't see many of the good things here. It's a mighty comforting thought," she added as she put the card back on the shelf, and went softly out.

Then, by and by, the housemaid made her late appearance, and paused in her frantic dusting of Madam's mantle-shelf, to look at the card. She paused so long that Madam ventured to ask what she thought it meant.

"Why, it just tells the blessed truth," she answered, "that even if the Savings Bank, with all you have in it, gets broke, so that you can't give the poor children so much as a bit of Christmas, yet the angels can tell us, if we would only hear them, that there's treasures laid up where banks do not break!"

So the little card grew richer all day to the poor Madam, as she heard its messages to the humble people about her; the same message, yet variously suited to their various wants, as God's truth always is.

Late in the afternoon, the minister who included crippled Madam on his list of poor, dropped in to see her. Of course she showed him her card, and was just wondering if she could dare ask of such a theological source what he thought of it, when he took the card to the window and read aloud the name in the corner.

"Dorothy Herman," he cried, coming back to the Madam, "Why, who is she?"

"She's the girl who painted the card," replied Madam, and proceeded to give Dorothy's little history—her arrival in America, the death of her father, and missing uncle. Suddenly there was a knock at the door, and Dorothy herself entered.

"Why, look here," cried the minister, "I'm just studying your name. I've got a little girl in my Sunday school, named Dorothy Herman, and her father is my organist. What was your uncle's name?" he continued.

"Carl Herman," answered Dorothy, quite pale with excitement, for she felt that something was going to happen, and it did, for on hearing this, the minister clapped his hands, and paced up and down the Madam's little room in the strangest way—urging Dorothy to run and get her things, for she must come with him, to a

Christmas Festival at his church that very night—
within the next hour.

A few moments later, Dorothy, hooded and
cloaked, took her way with the minister along the
bright, cold streets. They did not stop until they
reached the church all bright with light, holly
wreaths, and gathering members. Up in the choir
there was as yet only the organist fixing the lights
and music, and a little girl hovering about him.
Thither the minister and Dorothy made their way.

There was a moment's pause. Trembling,
Dorothy looked at the organist, and the organist
looked at Dorothy—then a cry, in the tongue of
the homeland, "My Uncle Carl!"

"My dear Dorothy!" They clasped in each
other's arms, while the minister stroked
astonished little Dorothy's hair and told her that
she would have to be called "Dolly" now, leaving
the older name for her new-found cousin.

After that, there were no more lonely, exiled
days for Dorothy. She entered at once into her
uncle's home, where she became a loving sister
to Dolly.

Madam's remaining days were among her
happiest, as she was soothed and helped by
Dorothy's sweetness, and brightened by Dolly's
sunshine.

Dorothy continued to bless the world with her
artistic conceptions of religious thoughts, though
her success in that way is now an old story.
Everyone knows that the famous prize cards with

"D. H." in the corner are hers; but not everyone knows the little history of this first one she so humbly designed for Madam. Very likely it still remains in heaven, as above them all—her Prize Card!

HUNTSVILLE, ALA.
[16 December 1885]

Song Of The Star

By Flake White

O winter star, with all your shining,
 Fill my heart with fire;
Another star, once, with its shining,
 Led the way to our Messiah!

O winter star, with all your shining,
 Fill my heart with light, I pray;
Another star, once, with its shining,
 Lit the world's first Christmas day!

HUNTSVILLE, ALA.
[21 December 1887]

Fables

Courtesy of The Weeden House Museum

"Courier of the Desert"
after Horace Vernet[1]
by
Howard Weeden

---

[1] [Emile-Jean-] Horace Vernet (1789-1863). A French painter known for his work depicting Arab subjects.

The Lost Diamond

Or, Effort and Achievement

There lived, once upon a long gone-by time, a certain King, who, in returning one day from an excursion into the desert bordering his kingdom, lost from his turban a diamond clasp of great value. A large reward being offered for its recovery, many of his subjects on swift horses and dromedaries set out to look for it.

Among those who undertook to search was a poor orphan boy, who held an humble place somewhere about the palace, and, mean as his station was, loved the king so truly that though he had neither friend, guide nor camel, he yet determined to make an effort in behalf of the lost gem.

His lonely journey toward the heart of the desert was occasionally varied by the passing of a group of camel-mounted noblemen, enlivening with jest and song their idle search. They would not even deign to glance over their cashmere-draped shoulders to look at the small, pale lad who slowly paced the desert alone.

A life of monotonous inactivity had rendered his young limbs weak and tender, but as he patiently bore the heat and weariness, his feeble sinews learned new strength and vigor, and his eyes acquired an eagle's keenness in searching the infinite sweep of sands. A spear, which he had found in the track of some wandering son of the desert, served as his staff and as a weapon against the wild beasts that often times crossed his solitary path.

Days passed by, and still the boy's patient eyes sought the sand unrewarded by the diamond's sparkle. Meantime, his journey had brought him into an almost unknown waste of the desert through whose deathlike barrenness travellers steered their camels, as they cursed the burning miles that contained no drops of water.

The guideless boy stopped and lay down amid this desolation, thinking to die of thirst. As he searched the sands that swept out to meet the burning sky for some sign of life, his glazed eyes began to close hopelessly. Moments later, a poor camel, apparently dying like himself, feebly dragged its gaunt body along the desert not far from him.

The boy was still lying in a sort of stupor some hours later when the same camel returned that way, no longer exhausted, but with a rapid and animated step and a look of renewed strength.

"He has found water," cried the boy, and starting from the ground, he staggered along the camel's track until it brought him at last to a little group of palm trees, with a shallow spring in their midst. He knelt and drank of the water. This spring, undiscovered until now, was hereafter to comfort and save many a wanderer like himself. Lingering a day or two beside it, he gathered some stones and with busy hands walled its precious waters in from the thirsty sand, sheltering it from the glaring sun. Then he set out on his search again.

Scarce ten miles of his journey had been accomplished when he came upon a group of richly equipped horsemen, who proved to be the King and a guard of knights returning from some journey. By the treachery of a guide, they had been left in this unknown stretch of sand and now gladly followed the confident tread of their stalwart young guide as he led them back to the "green and blessed" palm shade. The King and his knights raised a cry like a shout of victory when they gathered about the little well, and quenched their thirst in its sweet water, while the young discoverer stood by and told them the story of its finding.

The King seemed greatly pleased when he recognized in the intrepid youth the former servant of his household, and bade him speak more of his search for the diamond. But just then, a richly dressed knight, who lay beside the well and drank from a white, jeweled hand, scornfully informed the boy that his search had been in vain, as *he,* in the first day of his own search, had caught the glitter of the jewel in the sand and, without staying the speed of his horse, had caught the diamond clasp on his lance's point and returned it safely to the King. The patient boy looked wistfully at the indolent speaker for a minute, then bowed submissively and was silent.

"Call it not lost labor," said the King to the boy, "for I count your effort greater than this knight's achievement. He found the gem without pains, and so reaped no fruit. You searched in vain for the diamond, but found strength, sagacity, patience, endurance and longsuffering—virtues in a searcher that are beyond and above reward."

It is said to have been in memory of this young boy's search that the well was ever afterward called "The Diamond of the Desert."

[4 August 1869]   FLAKE WHITE

THE GARDEN OF DESTINY

The purple hills of Koh-i-noor* once threw their cool shadows across a garden that lay at their feet. Its radiant flowers, winding walks and pleasant shades, enlivened by the music of birds and the murmuring of the river that flowed by, rendered it a delightful spot. Its paths were worn by the tread of many young pilgrims, for it was the Garden of Destiny, and here, before passing the River of Care, they came to choose their emblems for life.

These emblem flowers were spread out in radiant profusion, but that their dazzling beauty might not mislead pilgrims, the Spirit of the Flowers stood forever near to give them counsel. The sun had just risen when a party of children from the hills of Koh-i-noor entered the garden. With timid step that gradually became bolder, they wonderingly walked amid the flowers.

"This," said a beautiful young girl, "is my choice, glorious beauty!" and in rapt admiration she paused before a Morning-glory that glowed and sparkled in dew and early sun.

"Daughter," said the Spirit, as the child gathered the frail flower, "the dew will soon leave it, and the noonday heat that will follow this early morning's coolness will rob it of its beauty."

Yet nothing else looked so fair to the young girl as she walked on with her choice. When an hour later its loveliness was gone forever, she wept bitterly, and threw it aside. "I will take none of these fair bright things," she said sadly, "they will all leave me like my glory." But as her tearful eyes glanced over the hosts of brilliant flowers, she saw amid them the pale gleam of a small white Immortelle which she gathered to her bosom, and slowly left the garden.

"This is my crest," said a boy, as he gathered a spray of Dragon flowers with their crimson lips and purple yawning jaws.

"See," said the Spirit, as she pointed to his hand all stained with the blood from the bruised flower, "your hands will always wear that hue though they bring you glory."

"Be it so!" he cried and left the garden.

"I shall live for the pleasure of the world," said another boy gathering a rich Pomegranate bloom. He crossed the flowing River of Care and was gradually followed by all the children except two.

The older of these, a boy, knelt before two flowers, a fair Lily with its stamens of dust-like gold, and a Hearts-ease. "This Lily will give beauty," he said thoughtfully, "and this little Hearts-ease. . ."

". . .will give contentment—the heart to look on the bright side of things," continued the Spirit, "for when beauty shall be as ashes, its spirit lives on."

The boy's sister stood near, looking earnestly at a fallen column, over whose timeworn crevices and black stains, Ivy was slowly and lovingly creeping. "To wear the Hearts-ease of happiness is good," said the Spirit, "but to wear the Ivy of charity that covers the defects of others is better far," and so with Hearts-ease and Ivy the two left the garden.

After crossing the River of Care, the road changed: the pilgrims' journey over the hills of Koh-i-noor had lain through flowers and over sunny slopes; now their young heads were bared to bitter storms and their tender feet to rough places and treacherous quicksand.

At last the weary journey was over, and so changed as to be recognized only by their emblems, the pilgrims stood before the Gate of Judgment. Upon this gate each child was to hang his emblem.

The pilgrim who had chosen the white Immortelle had gone silently and bitterly through her journey, stoically enduring the storms, and shutting her eyes to the fair things that were now and then scattered along the road. No new growth or grace had been given her flower; it bore only the brightness of "perished summers" and when she hung it upon the gate, it looked almost dead, as she passed silently through.

The two pilgrims with Dragon and Pomegranate flowers approached and hung them on the gate, but the opals of the gate seemed to flash back their crimson tints in a glow of fire until they fell as ashes. With a cry of despair these two children disappeared through the gate.

The pilgrim with the Hearts-ease stood radiantly happy before the gate; he had borne all the tempests and trials patiently, even joyfully; and so now passed singing beyond the gate. As his sister approached to hang her Ivy, a thousand voices, from glorified pilgrims on the other side as well as travellers still behind her—whose troubled spirits she had comforted, whose bruised hearts she had bound up, and of whose faults she had spoken pityingly—shouted her welcome. As Charity passed through the gate, she became lost in the stream of radiance that led to the Golden City.

*Mountain of Light   FLAKE WHITE
[3 May 1866]

The Jaybird And The Hawk
A Fable

A pair of jaybirds took up their residence one spring in a busy farmyard, where the spreading branches of a chestnut tree offered a fine place for their nest.

"We have come into a populous neighborhood," said the jay to his mate, "and while we may try to keep popular with our friends, we must not fail to keep even with our enemies."

The two chatting birds kept this resolution to the letter. And so, against the martins in the box, the swallows in the chimneys, the dog in the kennel, the cats, chickens, geese, ducks and foxes, they led a busy life. But the daily strife to keep even with their enemies so soured their tempers that they soon had no friends left with whom to be popular.

Wearied out at last one day with screaming, scolding and fighting, they both took refuge in the top of a lofty oak, and while resting there, saw above them sailing in slow, beautiful circles, a large hawk.

Presently the jays beheld several great, evil-looking birds approach and prepared to attack him. The slowly floating hawk took not the slightest notice of them till they got quite near, and then, without so much as the angry disturbance of a feather, he suddenly rose in the air, up and up, till he was lost from sight in the blue heavens! His dazzled enemies, baffled and defeated, sought the earth again.

"Behold," cried the jays together, "we have today seen the true art of attaining victory. To defeat one's enemies, one must not contend with, but rise above them."

[4 February 1880]   FLAKE WHITE

A GOLDEN NEEDLE

A Suggestion for the Work in 1897

BY HOWARD WEEDEN

Once upon a time, in that beautiful long ago —when Cinderella, Red Riding Hood, Jack of the Bean Stalk, Goody Two Shoes and such delightful people flourished—there lived a prince, so good and so lovely that he was always known as Prince Charming, and always deserved his name.

When he came of age to marry, his Fairy Godmother, who loved him devotedly, determined that he should have a wife, not beautiful and clever only, but as good and lovable as himself. So she set her fairy wits to work to learn all she could about the home-lives of the girls among whom he would probably look for a wife. The first thing she did was to offer a great prize for the best needlework done by any girl in the kingdom, and then, making herself invisible—as fairy godmothers know how to do—she went into all their homes, day after day, and watched them at their work.

Then a great entertainment was given at the palace, and hundreds of guests were there in their gala clothes. A great feast was spread, and the girls were bidden to bring the work they had done.

Never before was such beautiful sewing seen—great squares of the finest linen worked in silken violets, purple and white, and tied with enchanting love knots—and satin damask napkins embroidered with the Prince's coat-of-arms—and doilies enough to go round the world, worked in blue forget-me-nots to match (and catch) the Prince's eye—and drawn work beautiful enough to make the spiders ashamed of their webs—all were there. Fairy Godmother, Prince Charming, and the guests who did not strive for the prize, looked at the beautiful things and praised them to the skies.

Among the guests who seemed to admire and praise them most, the Prince noticed a young girl whom everybody was calling "Fair Margery." She seemed like her name, and he was devoured with curiosity to know why she had not contended with the other girls for his godmother's prize.

So at last he made bold to ask her the question; and she answered, smiling, that it was because she did not have the time.

"Did not have the time!" echoed Prince Charming, hurt and puzzled still; but before she could reply, Fairy Godmother drew near and spoke.

"What Margery says is true. I went invisible, into her home every day, as I did into other homes, and I saw her fingers never idle an hour, and it was mending—beautiful mending—she was doing. The darns were lovelier than any embroidered flowers, for they were the forget-me-nots of the heart! One day she would be darning a worn place in her father's old coat; another day a tear in a restless little brother's trousers—and there are two knees to every pair of trousers, you know; the next day it would be a rent in her tired mother's gown. This young maiden knows how life's friction makes many rents in life's vesture, and that for the comfort of each household, Love needs to be standing, always ready, with her golden needle threaded.

As the godmother ceased speaking, the Prince bowed low before the blushing Margery, and lifting an end of his silken sash, he tore it across, and smilingly said, "Wilt thou mend this some day for *me*, fair Princess?"

And this was the way Prince Charming got his wife.

And this was the way Fair Margery got the prize.

HUNTSVILLE, ALA.
[30 December 1896]

The Rose In A Prison

THE ROSE IN A PRISON

A Fable

A pink rose, blooming in a sunny garden, lifted its head one fine morning to a narrow window near which it grew, and looking in, saw on a table a beautiful white rose in a glass.

"Poor sister Blanche," cried Pink Rose, "how I pity your misfortune! Taken from your bright garden home, with its sunshine and sweet south wind, its flowers, bees and birds, and shut up in this prison to fade and die!"

"Don't pity me," answered White Rose gently. "My place is beside a sick prisoner, and my task is to comfort him. I have not left the summer behind—I have brought it with me. He looks at me and smiles, seeing in me a vision of all that once made the world so bright to him. He falls asleep, inhaling my breath—and still smiles in his dreams, as he babbles of green fields."

"It is so much better to give than to receive that I gladly resign all you enjoy, if my presence here gives but a single summer day to one from whose life the summer has fled."

[28 January 1880]   FLAKE WHITE

Courtesy of Mr. and Mrs. Jackson P. Burwell

"Softly now the light of day
Fades upon my sight away"[1]

by

Howard Weeden

---

[1] The Church of the Nativity in Huntsville, Alabama. The handwritten inscription on the watercolor is from a hymn written in 1824 by George W. Doane.

Titles Listed by Date

From 1866 to 1896, the *Christian Observer* published under various mastheads. They are abbreviated as follows:

CO: *Christian Observer*

COC: *Christian Observer and Commonwealth*

COFC: *Christian Observer and Free Commonwealth*

COPW: *Christian Observer and Presbyterian Witness*

COFCC: *Christian Observer and Free Christian Commonwealth*

COCC: *Christian Observer and Christian Commonwealth*

A chronological listing:

1. Patience, *COPW*, 8 February 1866:4.

2. Modern Fashions, Huntsville Daily *Independent*, 16 February 1866:2.

3. The Rock That is Higher Than I, *COPW*, 5 April 1866:4.

4. The Garden of Destiny, *COPW*, 3 May 1866:4.

5. Our Light, *COPW*, 14 June 1866:4.

6. Self-Denial, *COPW*, 30 August 1866:4.

7. The Old Picture, *CO*, 18 June 1868:4.

8. An Alpine Lad's Story, *CO*, 13 August 1868:4.

9. Fought and Won, *COPW*, 21 April 1869:4.

10. The Amen of the Stones, *COFCC*, 23 June 1869:4.

11. The Lost Diamond: or, Effort and Achievement, *COFCC*, 4 August 1869:4.

12. King Good-Gold and Little Good-Will: Two Christmas Fairies, *COFCC*, 22 December 1869:4.

13. The Scarlet Cloak, *COC*, 20 December 1871:3. Reprinted in *CO*, 23 December 1896:8.

14. Whispered Gifts, *COC*, 29 July 1874:3.

15. The Two Fortunes, *COC*, 9 December 1874:3.

16. Mrs. Browning's "Eve," *CO*, 16 June 1875:1. Reprinted in Huntsville Weekly *Democrat*, 1 July 1875:1.

17. A Ministry of Love: Let Your Light So Shine, *COC*, 22 March 1876:3.

18. Geraldine's Window: A Story of a Quiet Life, *COC*, 14 June 1876:3.

19. Geraldine's Window: A Friend in Need, *COC*, 21 June 1876:3.

20. Geraldine's Window: Phillis' Story, *COC,* 28 June 1876:3.

21. Geraldine's Window: Paul's Silhouette, *COC*, 12 July 1876:3.

22. The Blossoming Cross, *COFCC*, 25 April 1877:1.

23. A Plea for Pinafores, *COC*, 24 October 1877:3.

24. Redmond O'Hanlon: The Bag of Guineas, *COC*, 31 July 1878:3.

25. A Telltale Scrapbook, *COFCC*, 12 November 1879:3.

26. The Rose in Prison, *COCC*, 28 January 1880:3.

27. The Jaybird and the Hawk, *COCC*, 4 February 1880:3.

28. Household Decoration, *COFCC*, 29 November 1882:1.

29. Low and Lovely Songs, *COFC*, 6 February 1884:1.

30. Rev. Sam Jones at Huntsville: Letter to a D.D., *CO*, 18 February 1885:5. Reprinted in Huntsville *Independent*, 26 February 1885.

31. Nashville Art Exhibition, Huntsville *Independent*, 30 April 1885:3.

32. A Saturday Mission, *CO*, 8 July 1885:1.

33. A Christmas Card, *CO*, 16 December 1885:1.

34. Moody and Sankey at Selma, Ala., *CO*, 24 March 1886:5. Reprinted in Huntsville *Independent*, 1 April 1886:1.

35. The Work in Egypt, *CO*, 8 September 1886:1.

36. The Shut-In Travellers, *CO*, 12 January 1887:3.

37. Song of the Star, *CO*, 21 December 1887:1.

38. A Columbian Discovery, *CO*, 4 April 1894:20.

39. The Old Folk's Concert, Huntsville Weekly *Argus*, 17 January 1895:5.

40. Anton Rubinstein, Huntsville Weekly *Democrat*, 24 July 1895:3.

41. A Golden Needle: A Suggestion for the Work in 1897, *CO*, 30 December 1896: (1277).

About the Editors

Linda Wright Riley and Sarah Huff Fisk
finding Howard Weeden in the *Christian Observer*
at the *Louisville Presbyterian Theological Seminary.*

Sarah Huff Fisk co-authored, with Dr. Frances C. Roberts, *Shadows on the Wall: The Life and Works of Howard Weeden.* Fisk is a well-known writer and publisher of books about Huntsville, including *Civilization Comes to Big Spring: Huntsville, Alabama 1823.* She is past president of the Huntsville-Madison County Historical Society.

Linda Wright Riley earned her B.A. in English from Vanderbilt University where she won the Merrill Moore Creative Writing Award. While completing her M.A. in American Literature at the University of Southern California, she received the Sarah Graham Prize for literary research. Riley interprets Howard Weeden at the annual Cemetery Stroll sponsored by the Huntsville Pilgrimage Association.

❧ Order Form ❦

Lost Writings of Howard Weeden as "Flake White"

© 2005 by
Sarah Huff Fisk and Linda Wright Riley

<u>Enclosed is my check for:</u>

_____ Copies of the book at 22.95 each   =   _____

Alabama residents add 8% tax   =   _____

Postage/handling 2.50 per book   =   _____

Total   =   _____

<u>Please make check payable and mail to:</u>

Big Spring Press
701 Ward Ave.
Huntsville, AL 35801

<u>Book(s) to be mailed/shipped to following address:</u>

Recipient's name: _____

Street or P.O. Box: _____

City, State: _____

Zip Code: _____

Thank you for your order!